SEVEN SPIRITUAL STRATEGIES

How The Enlightenment Code Can Change Your Life?

You can now experience the highest state of freedom (without sitting in a lotus pose in a secluded cave in the Himalayas)

Sri Vishwanath

www.soulpowermagic.com

Copyright by Anantharaman Vishwanath

Seven Spiritual Strategies

All rights reserved.

First Printed in the United States.

No part of this publication may be reproduced, stored in a retrieval system, or transmitted, in any form or by any means, electronic, mechanical, photocopying, recording or otherwise, without the prior permission of the publisher or the author.

ISBN: 978-0-9847563-0-8

You can contact the author at vish@vish-writer.com. You can also reach him at his USA number at 2138142680. India contact number 91-22-21645009.

These are the type of comments the material in this book has gotten from those who have either read the manuscript or taken my online course

Bold! ...

Daring! ....

The Ultimate Truth ! ....

What used to take more than 12 years of disciplined practise can now be known, applied and experienced in less than eight hours. Thanks to the enlightenment code!

If a dumb person like me can know and practise these methods, then anyone can benefit from their life-changing, liberating and exhilarating manifestations!

It takes *Bhagavad Gita*'s teachings to the next level.

These messages are perhaps what Jesus Christ wanted to convey!

The Enlightenment code has also helped me understand the Qur'an better!

I could finally more fully appreciate Buddha's teachings!

My definition of religion has changed and become infinitely richer and clearer after coming in contact with the Ecode and fully conversant with its meanings! Five thousand years of accumulated wisdom are presented in an astonishingly simple manner!

I have emptied my book shelf ! The Ecode is all that I need !

Also by Sri Vishwanath

1) **Shakti** : The Greatest Secret To A Stress Free Life.

2) **No-Nonsense Meditation**: What The Greatest Wise Men & Women Knew About Human Consciousness That You Are Not Aware Of.

3) **The Joy of Becoming God.**

4) **Shraddha**: The Little Book on God.

5) **The Power Of The Vedas:** The Spiritual Guide That Has Been 5500 Years In The Making.

6) **The Story of Nachiketa** : How A Little Boy Conquered Death By Meditating On A Force Superior To Death.

7) **Give Up Your Excess Baggage:** 24 Simple Mind Exercises That Great Men & Women Effectively Use Every Single Day.

8) **Shiva:** Four Ancient Secrets To Win God's Grace.

9) **Zero Effort**: Maximising Potential With Ease.

10) **The Secret of Bhagavad Gita**

Dedication

TO LORD KRISHNA,
SRI RAMAKRISHNA, SWAMI VIVEKANANDA,
AND SRI SHARADA DEVI.

Acknowledgments

To my parents for teaching me spiritual culture

To my wife for teaching me purity of mind

To my son for teaching me the art of detachment

To life for being patient with me

To Krishna for being gracious with me

Table Of Contents   Page No

Chapter 1 – What is the Ecode?   10

Chapter 2 – The Seed of Extraordinary Transformation   18

Chapter 3 - The Art of Divine Connection   39

Chapter 4 - Invoking God to fulfill your wishes   56

Chapter 5 - The Power to Influence Your Destiny   75

Chapter 6 - Dancing with Maya(Illusion)   93

Chapter 7 - Kill the Old Mind   104

Chapter 8 – The Magic of the Ecode   114

Chapter 9 – The Mystery of Life & How To Demystify It   133

Preface

I have an interesting question for you.

Why do you think enlightenment should take you ten, twenty thirty years or a maybe a whole life time to attain? Why can't you realise it in less than, say, eight hours?

What is stopping you from being enlightened before you go to sleep tonight?

Have you ever thought about feeling enlightened and wondering why it seemed so elusive?

Which misguided person told you that it takes ages to get enlightened? Perhaps you misunderstood the ancient teachings of the prophets and founders of religions.

Enlightenment can be known, practised and experienced in less than eight hours. What takes a life time is maintaining that state of enlightenment.

Consider these profound statements:

- *First enlightenment, then laundry .-* Buddha

- *Neither by the Vedas(revered Hindu scripture) nor by charity nor severe penance nor austerities can I be reached. To the single minded yogin in perpetual communion with me I am always easily accessible.* – Krishna

- *And ye shall know the truth, and the truth shall set you free. Ask and it will be given to you; seek and you will find; knock and the door will be opened to you.* – Jesus Christ

- *One hour's meditation on the work of the Creator is better than seventy years of prayer.* - Mohammed

Read this book when you're most alert. Note that the first chapter is an introduction to the Ecode. Chapters two through seven contain illuminating stories that will stir the depths of your soul and set you up for embracing and uniting with the Ecode.

Chapter 8 contains the Ecode, which is likely to stun you when you realize its liberating elements. Don't jump to chapter 8 right away no matter how advanced a spiritual seeker you are. You'll blow away the opportunity to be free by the end of the day.

Don't stop reading while questioning anything written in the book, and avoid taking notes while reading. You'll remember everything that you need to know. Simply move on to the next page or chapter if you fail to absorb the essence of a particular chapter. The true meaning will become apparent shortly. You'll discover the Ecode when you are really in need of it.

Chapter 1

What is the Enlightenment Code?

Here is the big idea in 26 words: *It is the sovereign science, the sovereign mystery, and the best of purifiers. Its apprehension is immediate. It's righteous, imperishable, and easy to attain.* ---Krishna to Arjuna in the *Bhagavad Gita* (Song of God).

The enlightenment code has seven faces. When united they appear as one. When disconnected they appear as many. This book tells you why this disconnect occurs and how you can connect the seven dots with simple tweaks and achieve the ultimate state of realisation.

I Do Not Live In My Body

My spirit gets up at 4.00 am and goes to bed at 9.00 pm. My body sleeps in the night. My spirit loves Indian food and enjoys the little pleasures of life. My spirit doesn't read newspapers and watch television. It doesn't carry a mobile phone. Once in a while my spirit sits down and meditates. My spirit revealed to me the Ecode in less than seven seconds. My mind and body had kept it hidden from me for 39 long years. My spirit hates to call itself spiritual.

The Journey which I mistook to be a spiritual one

Like every other spiritual seeker I followed the rules, norms and the methods involved in this pursuit. I observed silence. I fasted. I went on holy trips. I chanted mantras for long hours. I meditated on the mystic symbols, read the best of spiritual books, and did everything I possibly could to outgrow my tiny personality. For a while all these activities seemed satisfying to some extent. I was proud to call myself spiritual until one day as I was about to leave to my work place my 11 year old son, Vignesh, came running to me and said: "Appa (Dad), I need your help."

"I will offer you the world. Tell me what you want," I replied

I have my math exam tomorrow and I can't solve a problem," Vignesh admitted.

I was pretty good in math and so I told my loving son, "No problem. Let's solve it together."

As I was showing him the right way to get the right answer my wife, Chitra, chipped in and said, " Vignesh, be careful of your father's method of teaching. It might contradict with your school teacher's method. Stick to your school teacher's method."

I laughed, confident that in less than 15 minutes I had helped my son solve this math problem which would aid him to get a good grade in his exam. The teacher, I thought, was looking to see if the student had the right answer, not how it was reached.

But as I was travelling to work I wondered, *What is important in life? The methods or the results?*

Why are so many of us confused and uncertain about our methods in seeking spiritual truth for ourselves? Why do we worry that we're trying to make an inferior method work? Why can't we focus on the results and allow our personality to choose the method rather than force an inferior method on a superior personality?

Consider: The more inferior the method the more time it takes to get to the results. The superior the method the faster you get to the results.

In this context, the Ecode is the superior method which will help you experience faster and more enduring results in striving for spiritual peace and serenity.

More than 10,000 hours of evolved thinking.

The Ecode is a discovery which took me more than seven years and more than 10,000 hours of constantly evolving thought. During this process I wrote ten best-selling books on spirituality, got admitted thrice to a hospital's intensive care unit, struggled with my personal goals, and had a troubled relationship. When the Ecode emerged in my mind all the storms in my personal life magically subsided, and I had to wonder just what had transpired.

Is this all real? Where have all my troubles disappeared? Where are my moments of frustration? Why is anger not lurking behind me? How could this be so easy? I have never felt so good., but will this this last for ever?

Who would believe me when I say I was enlightened without a guru and without having spent years in a Himalayan cave?

I had hit upon the superior method, and reached the ultimate destination. The superior method is all that you need to experience this sublime feeling. Everything else is secondary. The usual methods used to attract and inveigle you into the world of spirituality are inferior and should be recognized for what they are. But with the Ecode you're now on the right track and not likely to be ever derailed.

Enlightenment Seed No 1

It is the sovereign science, the sovereign mystery, the best of purifiers. Its apprehension is immediate, it is righteous, it is imperishable, and easy to attain. ---Krishna to Arjuna in the Bhagavad Gita.

What is meant by the sovereign science?

Among the sciences I am the science of the self, says Krishna. Krishna encourages us to go beyond the laws of the earth and embrace the laws of the spirit.

Accordingly, it's the sovereign mystery.

I am death carrying all beings away. Of things yet to be I am the origin, says Krishna. *Be not afraid of the mystery. The mystery of the soul can be unveiled, known, practised and lived through."*

Sovereign science is the best of purifiers.

Flawless indeed is the spirit hence the sages abide in it, says Krishna. *One touch, one embrace of the soul is sufficient to heal a million wounds of the past.*

In this sense, Krishna encourages us to be spirited and bold and to fear neither past actions nor present thoughts. Your divine nature is not so fragile to be influenced by a sinful thought or action.

Its apprehension is immediate.

Set your mind on me and let your understanding be absorbed in me. Henceforth doubtless shall you reside in me, says Krishna.

Understand that there is no evolution in the soul. The results are instant. You don't have to wait for ages to enjoy the rewards of embracing the spirit. What we call progress in spirituality is related to our innate development of the ignorant understanding of the soul. You can start connecting to your spirit right now and enjoy the fruits of your connection immediately.

It is righteous.

Enjoyments born of objective contacts end in pain only, Krishna explains. *They have a beginning and an end. The sages do not delight in them.*

Krishna encourages us to focus more on "righteousness" and less on good and bad, and right and wrong. Righteousness is a state of mind which creates the environment for appreciating the higher laws of the universe. Strive to be righteous at all times, says Krishna. Don't struggle with the spirit. It is futile. Simply embrace it.

It is imperishable

Him the fire cannot burn, the water cannot wet, the air cannot dry. says Krishna. *You cannot ignore the spirit. Eventually you will have to embrace it. Don't delay the embrace,* warns Krishna. *Your body and your thoughts might fail you with the passage of time but your soul never loses its sheen and power with time. Once touched it shines and glows for ever.*

It is easy to attain

Swami Vivekananda in his poem "In search of god" wrote:

A flash illumined my soul,
My heart of my heart opened wide
O joy O God what do I find,
My love my soul you are here and I was
Searching for thee everywhere for ages.

From that point on wherever I have travelled
I see Thee standing by...
Over hills and dales and mountain ranges
Far away and high...."

Krishna was the first religious figure who said: "It is easy to embrace the spirit and difficult to live without the spirit."

The spiritual life is the most enjoyable one, advises Krishna. In it you get an opportunity to manifest something you were always capable of. In this sense, Krishna says your body and the mind can help you achieve a lot of things; but you will be surprised with the depth of your thoughts and the calmness and radiance these thoughts can bestow in your daily life the moment you embrace the soul.

Everything is easy only if you know how.

Notes

....
....
....
....
....
....
....
....
....
....
....
....
....
....
....

Chapter 2

The Seed of Extraordinary Transformation

A huge spiritual tidal wave is coming... he who is low shall become noble, and he who is ignorant shall become the teacher of great scholars through His grace. – Swami Vivekananda

I want everyone reading this book to allow themselves the opportunity to become great. Do not belittle yourself with silly thoughts and with low vibrational energy. Know that you don't have to become great; you are born with something that is great and it's high time you start giving that thing the importance it deserves.

I want to start with an epic story from the *The Ramayana,* one of the two great epics of India (the other being the *Mahabharata).*

In the city of Ayodhya in northern India there lived King Dashrath. He had three queens, Kausalya, Kaikeyi and Sumitra. Dashrath was childless for a long time and so on the advice of his counselors he performed a fire sacrifice. As a consequence Ram – the hero of the *Ramayana* -was born to Kausalya; Bharath to Kaikeyi; and twins Lakshmana and Shatrughana to Sumitra.

All four boys excelled in archery, leadership and spiritual knowledge and there was mutual love and affection among them. As time passed by Ram was married to Sita and as King Dashrath grew old he expressed his desire that Ram the eldest of all and the most eligible be crowned as the king. All the people of Ayodhya loved Ram and wanted him to be crowned the king. Even the two other queens loved Ram.

However on the eve of his coronation terror struck

Queen Kaikeyi had a maid servant called Manthara who had an evil mind. While Kaikeyi was busy making arrangements for the coronation of Ram, Manthara slowly poisoned and planted the seed of dissent in Kaikeyi's fragile mind.

She praised Bharat who was the son of Kaikeyi and told her that while Ram is great it is Bharat her son who is greater and who deserved to be the king. Kaikeyi didn't pay much attention to her initially but Manthara kept repeating her terrible argument. At the tipping point Manthara reminded Kaikeyi of the two great boons which King Dashrath had once promised to the queen for saving his life.

Manthara convinced Kaikeyi it was time to ask the king to honor the favors he had promised her. The two boons were: **Your son Bharath should be coronated the king**, and the second **Ram should be sent into exile for fourteen years so that there is never a chance of his being the king again.**

Kaikeyi, by this time convincing by Manthara's sly comments, went to the king and requested both boons. King Dashrath was shocked but a promise made by a king had to be fulfilled.. He gave her many other options but Kaikeyi was adamant. Accordingly, the king called Ram and told him what needed to be done. But his heart was heavy and he fell at his son's feet and asked his forgiveness.

Ram, always level-headed, consoled his father without a murmur and urged him not to feel bad saying, He vowed he would come back in fourteen years.

Ram went to his palatial room, discarded all his royal robes, and donned the plain attire of a woodsman. He took his bow and arrow and requested that Sita, his wife, accept his departure.

"I go where Ram goes," Sita said. "I will follow you, my master."

At the same time Laxman Ram's brother, followed suit saying, "I will also go where my brother Ram goes."

Ram then proceeded to see his mother and get her blessings. Amidst grief and sorrow she blessed him. And then Ram did something which few would have the innate sense of compassion and forgiveness to do. He bowed before Kaikeyi and asked her blessings to complete his 14 years. Everyone at court was amazed by the extent of Ram's generous and noble nature.

Then Ram left to the forest accompanied by his wife and brother. What followed in the next fourteen years has been recorded as one of the most adventurous and thrilling epics in the history of the world. Every single trait of human character is revealed beautifully in this epic. I would encourage all of you to read the epic. There's also an animated movie *Ramayana - The Legend of Prince Rama* you might want to watch.

The reason I bought up the story was to emphasize that your mind is capable of being influenced by both evil and good. The wicked path of Manthara or the ennobling way of Ram.

Wise men and women don't pay much attention to the thinking patterns of individuals. They're aware that like spring goodness will rise and like fall evil will seep into the mind of many individuals. In the midst of all this change there is something that doesn't get disturbed or stir, and it is this crucial element that the wiser among us cultivate.

Think about it! If someone tells you to go exile for 14 years would you ask blessings from the person responsible for your banishment? Or would you slap and hate this person?

Why did the great Ram take Kaikeyi's blessings? What made him do that? Why was he so calm, was he not disturbed? What did he knew that you and I are not aware of ? Do such characters really exist or is it all a myth?

This brings us to Great Habit No 1.

Lean heavily on positive habits. When you pick up a healthy habit visualise the accumulated power that habit can have on your thinking. This is very important, and I want you to completely understand this concept.

Ask yourself these two questions

How can one small habit destroy decades of frustration and ignorance and completely transform my personality?

How much is my habit worth in dollar value?

If your habit isn't worth a million dollars don't establish and nurture this habit.

There are tons of million dollar habits waiting to be explored so don't waste your time focusing on the smaller ones. Think big and think boldly.

Don't form habits because everyone is forming that habit. Ask yourself: what will be the accumulated effect of this habit on my personality and my whole approach to life if I practise this one habit for a month, or for a year, or for fourteen years?

Work on only one healthy habit at a time.

If it's wealth that you're seeking, say to yourself in the first two hours of the day I'll shut all distractions such as working on the computer, handling phone calls, reading a newspaper, or watching the news on television. Instead, work on a strategy and follow that strategy to its logical end and on a daily basis. Put a brief description of this strategy on paper or an index card and where you'll be sure to see it every day.

You still might want to do things the way you have in the past, but remind yourself of what will happen if you follow your strategy – your new habit – for any length of time. Consider the good changes that will come to your personality, changes that you as well as other will quickly recognize and appreciate.

Say to yourself it's quite possible that I'll start slow but I'm confident that I'm moving in the right direction.

Dismiss your old mind and quickly

Say to yourself: "I don't care what I was earlier. I don't care what I did or what I am. I want to learn all the great things that life can teach and I want to learn them faster and quicker. My habits are worth a million dollars and I have confidence in my habits."

Don't look for shortcuts and show discipline. Play the game the right way. You might have to lose small battles to win the bigger ones, Allow yourself the privilege and latitude to do that.

Your habits should be worth at least a million dollars be it in wealth, relationships or health. You're a wise person

– even if you're not aware of it – and it's time that you should be cognizant of your innate abilities.

Practise this exercise after you get up.

The ideal time is in the morning because the energy of nature is high in the morning and the vibrations of the mind are at their peak. But if that isn't possible do the exercise at night.

Exercise No 1

Open your notepad and write five sentences or more everyday on: your ability to connect with your higher self.

What stops you from connecting to your higher self?

What encourages you to connect? What joy happens during connection?

Fill your notepad with lots of love and put your entire mind, body and soul into it. Take this assignment seriously for one week as the art of connection is the single most important skill before anything else.

Explore what "connection" means to you and as you progress you will be presented with that one big habit that can bring you a considerable measure of wealth either in terms of money, work, relationships, etc.

The great man think and you and I also think. But they think and their bodies follow...It is time we follow suit.

Each thought is a little hammer blow on the lump of iron of which our bodies are , manufacturing out of it what we want it to be" – Swami Vivekananda

It's worth rereading: Each thought is a little hammer blow on the lump and tissues of our mind. We can produce out of this mass what we want it to be.

You are born great! Have no doubt about it!

Enlightenment Seed No 2

The Power of Knowledge And The Weakness Of Concepts And How This Drastically Affects Your Thinking

Says Krishna to Arjun: *Deprived of knowledge as a result of cravings man tends to worship other deities and follow other disciplines being constrained by their inborn nature.*

Most people understand God through concepts. For example, Hindus think that if they know the various yoga techniques such as Karma, Jnana Raja or Bhakti are they then fully understand the messages of the *Bhagavad Gita*. They believe they can approach God. They make their own assumptions about these yogas based on their limited understanding of these concepts.

The same follows with other religion. Concepts, rituals, words and symbols used in the scriptures have been given more importance than the laws which these words or symbols were meant to express.

Knowledge is powerful only if you know where it is leading you to

Concepts are needed to understand a point but the very concept through which you understand something becomes the cause for your obstruction. Let me give you an example.

Open a notepad and start writing about "Love" ten minutes every day in the morning when you are fresh. Do this for two weeks. Write on a new page every day. At the end of the second week compare your notes of the last day with the first day's notes. What would you discover?

If you have gone through the process steadily you're likely to notice meaningful growth in the choice of words used on the last day of your writing compared to the first day. You might have started writing about love as a form of emotion or something you were seeking from others, and on the last day you might have talked about love in a totally different dimension where instead of seeking love you might have ended up writing about love as a channel for distributing or expressing your innate goodness to others. This is very much possible.

If you continue writing about "love" after two weeks you will break further barriers within yourself and take the expression of love to greater levels. You never know how your definition of "love" will develop and with everything that you write you will grow because you were the person who wrote on the first day and you are the stronger and wiser person who has continued writing it later.

You'll be surprised that when you put pen to paper and your mind and soul into the topic that hidden gems lying undiscovered within you will emerge. I promise you that. Take any topic be it God, love, compassion or anything else and if you're bold and innovative you'll derive the essence of that great idea.

Knowledge has to be approached step by step till the point that you're not 100 per cent intellectually satisfied

Once that is done it's a free line. Take the example of traffic lights. When you drive in the city you have to stop on many occasions as there are many traffic lights but once you hit the highway it's a breeze and there are fewer stops. Hold on to concepts till the time that you need them but be bold enough to leave them when you're ready to grow.

Ask yourself this simple question: Why are there so many different concepts and mysteries built around God?

If you ask many eighth grade school students about oxygen they have ready and correct answers. There are few mysteries surrounding oxygen. The element oxygen has been discovered and taught in schools and those who want to know more about it are free to explore the subject. Don't you think that if God too is approached in a step by step manner there would be peace and harmony and better understanding and respect for the creator of the universe? How can that be done?

The first step is to appreciate the higher laws discovered by philosophers and religious teachers in the past

These laws are not partial to any religion. They are simply higher because of their infinite wisdom. Higher laws aren't mystical in nature. They provide clarity and remove all confusion and doubt. If you find anything mysterious in spirituality or religion always remember to know the law behind the piece of mystery. Don't get overawed by the magic or spiritual majesty of these laws. Strive to know the aspects which make these higher laws appear so mysterious.

Think about it. If you ask some of the most intellectual people how the world started they're likely to have different and mysterious-sounding concepts. Don't you think that this is a sad state? Is creation so complicated that our intelligence can't comprehend it? What are we missing? The scientists approached creation as an event and so they went back in time and discovered the concept of the big bang. Spiritual and religious figures approached the subject as a mystery and wove their own concepts around it. But wiser people took a different route. They approached creation as a law, not as an event which happened millions of years ago or as a mystery which will continue to happen and keep us guessing.

Ask yourself these questions:

How can I think rationally? How can I think impartially?

How can I train myself to think with a broad mind?

So take up God as a study through laws and not through concepts, through love and not through anger, through inspiration not through dry intelligence

I want to share a story here. I had a habit of visiting a Krishna temple which was close to my house every morning and evening. This temple had strict rules that all men before entering the temple should remove their shirts, tshirts or anything else which they wore above their waist. So basically all men should be bare-bodied above the waist when they entered the temple.

One day when I was inside the temple and praying to God one of the men who was visiting the temple for the first time didn't read the rules properly and entered the temple wearing his shirt. And no sooner had he came in, three devotees inside the temple made a huge uproar. They held this man by the neck and dragged him out of the temple. I wondered what occupied the minds of the devotees who threw the man, only guilty of not reading the regulations carefully, out of the temple. Were they praying to Krishna or were they more interested in ensuring that others followed the rules of the temple?

Rules are important for the maintenance and continuity of any organisation but the regulations shouldn't become so important that one forgets the higher laws which these rules were meant to support. There are many such incidents which I encountered during my visits to temples in India and I can't help wondering how people fall prey to the various rules and make them look so big.

Next in line comes the magical things. Walking on water, flying through air, reading a person's mind, manifesting an object instantly, making dead people alive. In this sense, Krishna reveals: *Do not fall for the millions of magical and mystical things happening on earth. They do more harm than good. Be calm enough to observe the great law working in the background and attempt to move closer towards that higher law.*

Here's another interesting story. Once the great Buddha was travelling around India with his disciples and camped in a village. In this village there was a mystical person who used to manifest physical objects from thin air. One of Buddha's disciples happened to meet the person and the mysterious person manifested a big vessel from thin air and gave it to the disciple. The disciple very happily came to Buddha and narrated the strange incident. Buddha took the vessel from his disciple, put it on the ground, and crushed it with his feet.

Faith should never be based on miracles, Buddha declared.

Faith is an effect. It isn't the cause for inspiration. Faith develops as a result of healthy thinking, mature behaviour, and a boldness to broaden your personality in the right direction. The faith which is apparent in the world right now isn't faith. It's foolishness, a dumb and meek approach to moving towards the wonderful architect of the universe. If only the world knew what faith could achieve it would not talk loosely about it.

The power of simple questions
What is the objective of asking a question?

The objective of asking a question isn't to find an answer to the question but to move towards a finer question.

When we move in this direction we will be left with very few questions or only one question. That is how great minds work. Such questions as how you can get rid of your anger or change a certain attitude won't lead you anywhere. A wiser approach is to know the source of these questions and that is what Krishna reveals when he says we are bound by our nature and our nature forces us to ask questions. You are not your nature. Your nature is influenced by your past thoughts and you're not your past thoughts.

If you observe all your thoughts you'll soon find out that your thoughts are influenced by your environment both physically and mentally.

It's like attending a funeral and asking respectful questions to the relatives of the departed ones because we're there in that sad environment. We may not be totally serious or sincere about the departed ones. We ask the pro forma questions and then move on with life.

Our questions don't lead us anywhere

Krishna advises that we shouldn't waste our time asking needless questions and getting buried in the concepts.

Don't think that if you know what karma or bhakti yoga are that you will know God. Don't think that if you know what resurrection is you will know the greatness of Christ. That approach, propagated for ages, is false. Instead, ask yourself simple questions: What can I learn in Karma yoga which can help me to unite with Krishna.

How will resurrection help me to embrace the divinity of Christ?

God is a connection. It is a deep knowing, and not intellectual gymnastics.

My intention in this book is to remove the scars and cobwebs of concepts which have been hammered into your minds for thousands of ages. I don't want to make the mistake of interpreting the scriptures. It would be a big mistake if I attempted to do that.

Your day to day activities should not steal your happiness

Organise your routine tasks, but don't give the daily tasks more importance than they deserve. I know how it hurts. It takes away our life. Place everything in this world that is routine in sensible perspective and focus on connecting with everything that is divine. Be serious about your connection with God. Let that be your first priority with everything else secondary.

Says Krishna to Arjun: *Fix your mind on me, be my devotee, let your understanding be absorbed in me, thus moving ahead you will reach me for you are dear to me.*

Remember you can't find happiness in your day to day activities. Happiness is discovered when you have mastered the art of connecting with the divinity within you. Once you do that all the activities that you perform won't create a mental strain on you. You'll be energetic fresh and cheerful even after a whole day's work.

Don't be afraid when it comes to knowing God

Make your mistakes but don't be silly enough to fear that if you do something wrong God will punish you. If that was the case we all should have been born deaf and dumb. An average human being thinks many thoughts during a day and some or many of them are foolish, selfish, wicked and harmful. Always take the support of higher laws and grow with them. Don't be under the false impression that because you didn't follow a certain ritual on a particular day or didn't pay respect to God on a festival day it will harm you. Stop this nonsensical thinking!

God isn't a human being with a limited mind. He is intelligence personified.

Says Krishna to Arjun: He is both outside and inside, he moves not and yet he moves. Since he is subtle it is difficult to understand him .He is near and yet very far.

There is nothing in this universe which is without God. - Vedas

Adds Krishna: He is not lost to me who beholds me everywhere and who beholds everything in me neither am I lost to him. All beings dwell in me but I dwell not in them.

Krishna says he didn't create the universe but that he became the universe. He didn't create good and bad things; he created you.

You created good and bad things and got attached. You are complete but the good and bad things are incomplete. Let me give you an example.

Let's say you invented a popular video game. The rules of the game are that if you kill 100 people you get 100 points, and if you save 100 people you will get 1000 points. Are you as the owner of the video game affected by the computerized killing and saving of people? Answer this question please.

Consider that you may not be affected but the people playing the game will go through various emotions, not all of which are necessarily good. In fact, it doesn't affect players either. They may just stop playing at any point, realizing that it is after all a game and they are superior to the game. In this respect, Krishna says that you are greater than your emotions, and that you are greater than your current circumstances. You are greater than even nature

Look at what power Krishna put in our hands! Amazing! Look at what great sages have discovered for us. They gave us answers to everything.

The only question which has remained unanswered is: Why did God create the universe? This question will remain a mystery and rightly so because it doesn't deserve an answer. Any answer would be a guess and should be avoided. Why God created the universe is equal to asking why did the owner of the video game create the video game? You can discover that only if you are able to get into the minds of the owner of the video game. Similarly, when you merge with the divine you would have discovered that truth; but when you discovered it you would have lost the capacity to express it as you would no longer appear in a form. You would have become one with the unmanifest.

So the question why the unmanifest became manifest doesn't make sense. So long as you know that the manifest will return back to the unmanifest you have discovered the ultimate truth.

Reveals Krishna: *The beginning is unmanifest, the middle is manifest and the end is unmanifest, O Arjuna. There the sun shines not nor the moon much less the earthly fire that is my abode reaching which none returns back, O Arjuna.*

People with limited minds think: **Is God really concerned about the world?**

I had written a book two years back titled *Shraddha:Everything you wanted to know about love and God* and I had approached the word "God" in a humorous and completely different manner. I want to reproduce certain texts from this book relating to the topic "Is God really concerned about the world? I'm sure you'll enjoy them.

1) God doesn't misuse His powers. He didn't invent a nuclear weapon to safeguard Himself. He left that job for top nuclear scientists on earth.

2) God isn't sitting in an office and having fun watching all the antics of the world.

3) God allows himself to be cursed when there is a large scale destruction on account of an earthquake, a terrorist attack, or death of a loved one.

4) God doesn't take credit when a human being becomes successful, when a hospital is built, or when two kindred spirits love each other.

5) God doesn't want the world to change. He wants you to evolve.

6) God is in a dilemma. In the next two seconds something horrible is going to happen. He needs your help in finding a solution. He wants you to go through the list of future events below and suggest a suitable line of action.

a) A group of terrorists are about to blow a major five star hotel in Mumbai. Some 844 people are expected to die in this tragedy.

b) A wicked man is about to lure a 21 year old innocent women into a life of vice.

c) A thief is about to steal the life savings of an old man who just returned home after withdrawing money from the bank.

d) A pure man who has led a life of integrity and honesty is about to commit a crooked act.

e) Three teenagers are about to get together and plan an evil act for the first time in their life.

f) Your child who is crossing the road this moment is about to be hit and killed by a drunken truck driver.

All the events above are expected to take place in the next two seconds. If you had one second to react which event will you avert? You would obviously save your child. Well, that isn't what God might have done. In fact, it could be possible that He might not have interfered with any of these horrible events above. One of the important things that you have got to realize before you point fingers at the intelligence of God is: your order of importance in dealing with the issues of the world is quite selfish as can be seen from your choice in the above example. Human beings can only see the world through their own interests; they don't have the ability to observe the world as it is.

God doesn't carry any emotions

It's important that you understand this. If he did He would never have allowed any bad event to take place on earth. God is all intelligence. This intelligence can never falter. Never - that is the word. Our minds are too small to think beyond the realm of our desires.

7) God doesn't have the power to undo a human act. He doesn't even attempt to do that. He only gives you a better opportunity to grow.

8) Remember God laughed when he created human beings and wept when he gifted them with a thinking mind.

Notes

....
....
....
....
....
....
....
....
....
....
....
....
....
....

Chapter 3

The Art of Divine Connection

The world and all things in it are valuable; but the most valuable thing in the world is a virtuous woman. – Mohammed

I'm going to present two stories which are in complete contrast with each other and yet they blend themselves beautifully. The first one is the story of Sage Tukaram.

Sage Tukaram was born in India in a small village in the state of Maharashtra. The funny thing about sage Tukaram was outwardly he was just like everyone else. He was married, had a child, and he did few things for a living. However, he had one supreme quality - he was connected at all times to the divine.

Tukaram was very generous and used to give away whatever he had without even thinking for himself or his family.. Tukaram's wife didn't like this. She used to yell at Tukaram on many occasions, even hurl abuses at him for his overly generous attitude.

Tukaram owned a small sugarcane field and one day after a whole day's work he collected all the sugarcane and set out to sell them. Singing the name of Krishna as he was walking with this small cart of sugarcane he came across a big group of people who were very poor and had not eaten for many days.

Seeing them Tukaram forgot about himself and his family and he distributed the sugarcane to those poor people.. When he came home he had little left. His wife was furious. "Where is the money? How will I feed our son? Have you gone mad?"

And in a burst of anger she threw a stalk of sugarcane at Tukaram. It struck his head and fell to the ground in three pieces.

Tukaram was overjoyed and he thanked Krishna "Krishna, you are great. We are three people, myself my wife and our son, and now you divided that one sugarcane into three."

A few years later when sage Tukaram became a force to reckon with in spirituality he was asked, "You are such a great sage but look at your wife who abuses you before everyone else."

Tukaram replied, "When I don't have any problem with my wife abusing me why are you bothered?"

What a reply by the great sage!What did that great man knew that you and I don't?

He was aware completely of the law of karma. Many think they know this law but very few know it deeply.

When you know something completely conflict ends

When knowledge isn't complete doubt lingers; action is delayed and becomes ineffective.

Tukaram knew that his greatness was because of his past and his immediate problem with his wife is also because of the past. He knew that the attitude of his wife towards him wasn't a permanent problem. It was a temporary one and would end when the effect of the past simmers down.

He wasn't bothered about his immediate problem. He was concerned only about one thing - his connection with the divine. That's the only thing which we have freedom over.

Tukaram was aware of the greatest secret which Krishna revealed to Arjun

Stop thinking. Start connecting.

Thinking puts you in the past. Connection helps you enjoy the present and prepare yourself for the future. When you connect you lose the ability to think. You discover a higher power than the ability to think. You come in contact with high vibrational energy which makes you feel good, powerful and peaceful.

When you're connected, everything that you think might appear as a thought; but these thoughts aren't influenced by your past impressions. They're independent and not the result of your past behaviour, character or knowledge. They stem from a source which is complete.

Tukaram knew that he couldn't do anything about the attitude of his wife even though he was a sage. Even if he possessed higher powers he didn't consider it appropriate to play with the law of karma.

The law of karma is a higher intelligence.. It will work its way around. It ensures that every subtle cause is brought to a tangible result.

Wise men and women are aware of the law of karma. They don't meddle with it. They allow karma to produce its result. They don't feel bad about things which go wrong over which they have no immediate control. They're well aware of the secret that the law of karma works its way through a human thought and forces one to take action and thereby producing the result.

The thought is the strength of the law of karma

Hence Krishna advises: Stop thinking. Start connecting. We're puppets as far as the workings of karma but we make our own destiny when we learn the ability to connect. Our destiny began with the search for that "wonderful thing" and we got stuck in between. We have to reclaim our destiny.

All destinies culminate with the union to higher self. You can't do anything about your present character or circumstances. They're influenced by your past thoughts and actions.

You, however, have one choice today. Instead of struggling with your circumstance or character, train yourself "to connect." Drop the word "thinking" from today and start using the word "connect." With family, friends and colleagues learn the ability to connect. Develop that skill.

Sage Tukaram was aware of the power of connection. He won in the end and his wife became his disciple. It took him 12 long years to wear out the law of karma. During this period both he and his wife went through pain. However, their approach towards pain was different. His wife had to struggle with him because she was ignorant of the higher laws while Tukaram braved the odds in boldly attempting to practise the higher laws. He had come to show humanity that an immediate trouble shouldn't be abandoned or carried forward.

Tukaram was aware that if he had left his wife he would have encountered the same pain through other means. If his wife had left him during the struggling phase she would have probably married another man and the misery would have continued in a different form.

They won in the end because the power of connection of Tukaram was more powerful than the law of karma... period.

Let's move to the next story.. The story of that great man whom half the world used to worship at one time, Gautama Buddha.

His story is in complete contrast to that of Sage Tukaram.

Siddhartha(who later became known as Gautama Buddha), a prince of the kingdom, one day left his wife and children and went to the forest. He wanted to meditate on what was more important than all the worldly concerns.

The law of karma forced Siddhartha to die and Buddha to emerge.

The law of karma had made the thinking mind of Siddhartha redundant. He had consciously connected to that great energy called Buddha. He stopped thinking like Siddhartha, and started connecting like a Buddha... even before his teachings spread.

Every wise person has made use of this tremendous skill of connecting. It's your chance to follow suit.

Ordinary minds can't understand the power of great men and women. They don't pay attention to the social protocols of the world.

Said Buddha many years later:

When I left the palace, my father (the king) was told that I was doing a great wrong in renouncing the family. My parents, kinsmen and others tried to put pressure on me to return to the ties of family life. These wrong efforts on their side made me more determined to pursue the spiritual path. In the quest for spiritual peace several ordeals have to be overcome. Today I have found the Truth about life. What is it?

The sanctification of the five senses is the way to Truth. If the senses are polluted, of what avail are spiritual exercises? When the water in a tank is polluted, all taps will only give polluted water. Your heart is the tank. When it is filled with good thoughts and feelings, all that comes out of the senses - your speech, your vision, your actions - will be pure."

Train yourself to stop thinking about attaining prosperity, having better relationships, and enjoying good health and instead master connecting. Remember always that when you think you're influenced by the law of karma.

When you connect and then think you're still affected by the law of karma but know that you're not influenced by it. Your thoughts are independent of your past behaviour. You don't pay much attention to the current circumstance and the attitude of people around you. Your focus is on freedom and the channel of freedom lies solely on your ability to connect.

Tukaram didn't pay attention to the rude behaviour of his wife. Buddha wasn't concerned about his breach of social protocols and his responsibilities as a prince. They gave up everything for the joy of connecting. They gave up thinking about all the abuses, all the sufferings, and all the hardships that were to follow.

They were aware of the law of connection. How about you?

I have a simple exercise which will bring good results.

Exercise No 2

Take up one area of your life which needs attention. It could be a relationship, wealth, health, etc. Now take your notepad. Divide your page into two and on the right hand side of the page write down three things which are disturbing your mind relating to your chosen subject.

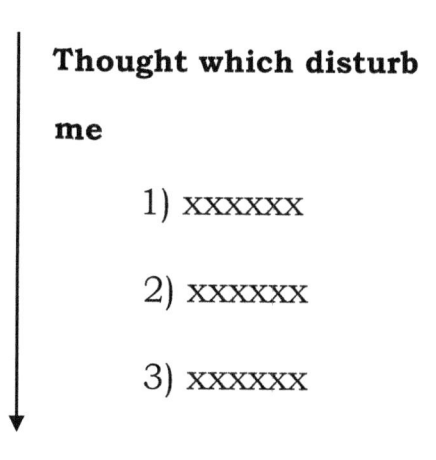

Thought which disturb me

1) xxxxxx

2) xxxxxx

3) xxxxxx

Now take your pen and strike out all the three concerns or issues. Let it all go. Kill your ability to think about these issues. Set your mind free and connect.

Write down three ways which will help you to connect with your higher self.. Focus on the channels of connection. Come up with innovative ways of staying connected.. List and follow them.

The Joy of Connecting	**Thought which disturb you**
1) xxxxxx	~~xxxxxxxxx~~
2) xxxxxx	~~xxxxxxxxx~~
3) xxxxxx	~~xxxxxxxxx~~

↓

There is only one thing which stands between you and Krishna. Just one thing which stops you from embracing the spirit of Christ. Just one thing which illuminates the dictums of Buddha.

The ability to connect! Connect freely and lovingly, and do it today!

Enlightenment Seed No 3

The Secret of Change

You can start implementing today the two skills that Krishna revealed to Arjun.

The word "God" is a discovery which happened after human beings exhausted their entire energy fulfilling every single desire of their mind. Great men and women appeared and disappeared but the majority of humanity have struggled with the word "God".

Reveals Krishna to Arjun: *Even if a person of wicked conduct worships me exclusively he is indeed deemed worthy for his resolution his right.*

Grow up, says Krishna. A wicked man is greater than the temple, church and mosque. The purity inside the temple, the divinity inside a church and the holiness within a mosque is inferior compared to the unmanifested energy lying dormant in a wicked person.

Look at the power Krishna hands out to you. He says human beings are purer than all his own idols which are worshipped every single day on earth.

Krishna wants you to grow, not the idols.

If a temple is built the purity of that temple should arouse at least a hundred great men and women, says Krishna. If one church is built at least a dozen giants like Christ should emerge from the society. If one mosque is built brotherhood, love and affection should glitter in that city.

Look around and you'll discover that this isn't the case. We're simply pampering the gods and weakening our own self. The idol of Krishna is given more importance than the teachings of Krishna. The names of Christ and Mohammed have helped many to become super-rich and famous while the character of those great men bite the dust.

The energy of the society is a clear indication of where we stand.

The powerful men and women who run countries and the world might be able to influence the minds of millions but they lack the capacity to manipulate the divine energy working in the background.

The Secret of Change

Krishna reveals: *Purusha lodged in Prakarti experiences the constituents born of Prakarti. The cause of the birth in the womb good or evil arises as a result of holding on the constituents of change.*

Krishna declares that discussing "change" is a waste of time. It's more fruitful to discuss and remember that which isn't influenced by anything and which can never change.

Let's try a simple exercise. Can you experience the warmth of summer while walking on a cold winter night? Can you force the arrival of summer during winter?

Think about it. We struggle with the nature of our thoughts every day. Every moment we are trying to express ourself better. We attempt to overcome the obstacles which we face. We're trying to change.

Krishna asks you to step back and give up the desire to change

He reveals that instead of fighting with change hold on to something that never changes. Your struggle with change will cease the day you discover and hold on that wonderful unmanifested energy which causes all change. Purusha is the unmanifested energy and Prakarti is a manifestation of purusha which influences the change.
Purusha is real. Prakarti is apparent. The cycle of creation is real and the seasons are apparent. One who knows that summer will follow a winter won't unduly worry about summer and will make preparations during winter for a great summer. Krishna encourages you to do the same.

Don't struggle with change. Embrace that which never changes.

Every morning after you get up simply do two things.

1) **Remember Purusha**.(the real) Acknowledge that you are great no matter how horrible your current circumstances are. Say to yourself that "You are greater than all the idols in the temples, all the churches, mosques and every other place of worship." Say it boldly. Gods in heaven will be happy when you do that. Krishna, Christ Mohammed, and every other founder of a religion will rejoice when you practise this. Simply feel happy that you own something which can never be destroyed and which can never be influenced. Feel and experience it!

   Reveals Krishna: *An eternal part of my being has become the Jiva in the world of beings. It pulls the senses together with the mind as the sixth which are set in Prakarti.*

Krishna reveals that the Purusha has become the jiva in you. The jiva stands for the individual soul and the purusha for universal soul. You're the jiva and the manifestation of Purusha. Rejoice.

2) Observe Prakarti (the apparent, that which is subject to change)– Krishna reveals that you don't need to change Prakarti. Simply observe it. You can't change Prakarti. Krishna teaches that that you can only attempt to influence Prakarti but in the end Prakarti will reign supreme. Great men and women came and disappeared but evil crookedness and wickedness prevails in the world. Krishna says to pay attention to the cycle of creation. There will be times when every human being will be pure, straight- forward and lovable; and there will be times when most of the human beings will be crooked and evil will dominate. This is the law of nature.

Krishna declares: *Whenever virtue subsides and irreligion prevails I manifest myself again and again. I balance the world not you. Do not meddle with the laws of nature. Work with it. Do not attempt to change the world. No one has succeeded so far and none will in future.*

If you have a great intention Krishna says to work for the good of the world, but remember that if you force summer during a cold winter you'll only get frustrated. Work because you feel good helping others. Think clearly and rationally because that's your nature. Be straightforward because you can't help being that way.

Observe everything that changes, says Krishna. *Prakarti is the cause which accomplishes all effects, O Arjuna.*

Observe the workings of your mind. How you are calm one moment, angry the next moment, loving for some time, selfish for a while. Observe your mind but don't struggle with it.

Krishna says don't feel bad if you think crooked, selfish and low thoughts

The thoughts are simply a reflection of your current personality, not your real nature. The moment you remember Purusha everything will disappear and that aspect of your personality which isn't subject to change will dominate. It's as simple as that. If you observe the erratic waves you'll become identified with the waves. If you transcend your identification to the ocean and merge with the serenity of the ocean the nature of the waves will no longer bother you.

Krishna warns us not to get fooled by the nature of our thoughts and attempt to change them. Krishna says simply to change your identification. Allow your thoughts to be merged with the source from which all thoughts manifest themseles.

You might have thought a million selfish thoughts until now but remember there's something within you which never got affected even after you produced all these negative thoughts.

You might have lusted a million times until now but remember there's something within you which never got affected even after you desired many women.

This is the reality. This is the truth. This is what wise men and women termed as "God." Move closer to it and you will discover its essence.

Set your mind on me be my devotee, pay austeries to me, thus striving forward you will surely reach me for you are dear to me, O Arjuna.

I would encourage you to read the poem "Hold on yet a while Brave Heart" by Swami Vivekananda which I have reproduced below.

"Hold on yet a while Brave Heart" by Swami Vivekananda

*If the sun by the cloud is hidden a bit,
If the welkin shows but gloom,
Still hold on yet a while, brave heart,
The victory is sure to come.*

*No winter was but summer came behind,
Each hollow crests the wave,
They push each other in light and shade ;
Be steady then and brave.*

*The duties of life are sore indeed,
And its pleasures fleeting, vain,
The goal so shadowy seems and dim,
Yet plod on through the dark, brave heart,*

With all thy might and main.

*Not a work will be lost, no struggle vain,
Though hopes be blighted, powers gone ;*

Of thy loins shall come the heirs to all,
Then hold on yet a while, brave soul,
No good is e'er undone.

Though the good and the wise in life are few,
Yet theirs are the reins to lead,
The masses know but late the worth ;

Heed none and gently guide.

With thee are those who see afar,
With thee is the Lord of might,
All blessings pour on thee, great soul,

To thee may all come right!

Notes

Chapter 4

Invoking God to Fulfil Your Wishes

If a person who lives in God becomes miserable, what is the use of living in God? What is the use of such a God? Throw such a God overboard into the Pacific Ocean. We do not want such a God! – Swami Vivekananda

In the last two chapters we explored the word "connection" and why "the ability to connect" is many times superior than the "ability to think."

In this chapter I'm am going to walk you through two contrasting stories of what "powerful connection" can really help you achieve and how it can dramatically influence, improve and help you get rid of mental blocks.

The first story is of a wise man named Aditya who lived in a tiny village in southern India 150 years ago. He was very learned, a master in spirituality and an authority in interpreting scriptures. He was married and he made a living by helping people sort out their daily problems and providing answers to many of their subtle questions relating to God and spirituality.

Then one day famine struck that village. Within a few days the entire village had nothing to live upon. It was completely barren. Most of the villagers had gone broke. Aditya's wife was concerned about how her family would survive... However, Aditya was busy interpreting the scriptures which was quite annoying to his wife.

There was very little food to eat and dutiful as ever his wife prepared hot food for him from the food stock remaining and requested him to come and eat.

However, Aditya had his head buried on one interpretation of Krishna's wisdom which read:

To beings who exclusively meditate on me and who worship me elaborately, and who incessantly apply themselves to meditation I carry for them prosperity and security.

Aditya was furious with the author who he felt had interpreted the *Bhagavad Gita* wrongly. He was very angry and thought: *It is impossible that Krishna will carry prosperity and security to his exclusive devotees. Does Krishna have no other work than to carry it personally to all his devotees? It is impossible.*

He took his writing instrument and struck out the word "carry" three times and replaced it with "grant." .Aditya had a furious temper and he started yelling at his wife too about the mistake which the author had made.

"Krishna does not carry prosperity himself," he told everyone. "He only presents and grants opportunities which can help the right devotee to seek prosperity and security."

Meanwhile, the village was still barren as a result of the famine and it had become very hot. His wife wondered, *We have nothing to eat for tomorrow and my husband is more worried about a mistake which isn't going to help us solve the problem of food.*

"We have no food for tomorrow, master" said his wife. "I suggest you go to the landlord of the village. He has plenty of food grains and will surely help you."

"I will, I will,".... said Aditya before leaving for the landlord's house. But then he added, "You people are more interested in food. You don't understand the gravity of the mistake committed by this author."

Aditya's wife was very devoted to Krishna. She didn't have the power of interpretation and the ability to express the subtle knowledge the way her husband could; but she had one important quality she had nurtured all through the difficulties - the ability to connect.

She picked up the scripture where her husband had struck out the word "carry" and had replaced it with "grant." *How could that be possible,* she said to herself. *I'm sure that Krishna does come personally and rewards his devotees with prosperity of their choice.*

Before her stood the idol of Krishna which she and her husband used to worship everyday... With her eyes fixed on the serene presence of Krishna she said. "I think Krishna does come personally. I am convinced that Krishna would come. Come Krishna, I need your help today."

She looked out of her balcony. The village was silent without a villager in sight. It was dry and hot outside. As she kept looking, and her vision transcended beyond the immediate sight, she heard a melodious voice from a distant place. It sounded like the song of a little boy singing.

How could that be possible? How could someone sing so joyfully in such heat when no one would even dare to walk on the street?

Was she dreaming?

With every passing minute the song of the little child burst open the little pockets of knowledge of Aditya's wife. She was pounding with excitement to meet this little child. How much joy she felt in just hearing his voice!

Five minutes later the voice presented itself in a form. The little boy was standing in front of her house with a big basket of delicious fruits—juicy mangoes, bananas, oranges and a variety of other foods.

"Please accept this basket of fruits and food." said the little boy with a twinkle in his eye.

Aditya's wife could not believe it. It's impossible. It wasn't meant for her.

Seeing the confusion in her mind the little boy clarified, "The fruit basket is all yours. I have been instructed to deliver this to your place by my master. Please accept it. I have to leave."

Saying so the little boy left the place.

As the little boy turned his back on Aditya's wife she saw three distinct marks of someone having hit him very harshly on his back.

How could someone be so cruel and hit him so badly, wondered his wife. *Could her husband be the one who had hit the little boy? It's very much possible that my husband could have hit him because the landlord wouldn't have given him the food grains and he might have shown anger and forced the child to deliver the fruit basket to our house. How cruel of my husband!*

Before she could come out of her world of imagination the little boy had disappeared and she couldn't ask him any questions.

Hesitatingly, she took the fruit basket inside her home and waited for her husband to return.

Twenty minutes later her husband walked in empty handed and her suspicion was confirmed. She started yelling at him instantly saying how he could do that to a little boy. "Why did you beat him and force him to deliver the fruit basket?"

Aditya thought the outside heat had made his wife mad. He didn't reply and went to his room. As he entered the aroma of juicy mangoes sent a wave of fresh energy inside his empty stomach. His eyes fell on the fruit basket filled with the choicest of fruits.

In a second what had happened dawned on him. He hurried to pick up the scripture where he had struck out the word "carry" three times. And there the verse: *To beings who exclusively meditate on me and who worship me elaborately and who apply themselves incessantly to meditation I carry for them prosperity and security, O Arjuna.*

Aditya realized that the deleted part of the scripture had disappeared from the scripture the moment he became aware that his ignorance of the "power of connection" had resulted in the three lashes seen at the back of the little boy.

The word "grant" wasn't seen in the scripture any more. The word "carry" shined in its true splendour. Krishna had come in the form of a little boy. Aditya, supposedly a scholar, felt humbled.

The power of connection had triumphed!

What did Aditya's wife knew that Aditya had failed to grasp? The key word is "exclusive." Let's go through that verse again

To beings who exclusively meditate on me and who worship me elaborately and who apply themselves incessantly to meditation I carry for them prosperity and security, O Arjuna.

His wife had exclusively connected with Krishna. It wasn't a blind belief. She was aware of the law of karma and she wasn't stupid to have been carried away by the law of attraction gimmicks which we see in today's world.

Her connection was straight and direct. She didn't believe in miracles but she had exclusive faith in the power of her connection with Krishna.. She had never asked Krishna for anything till that point and even on that day all she wanted was Krishna to come and help her mentally. She didn't ask for a basket of fruits or money.

Ask and ye will be given, said Christ.

Believers are serious when they say that. Yet one should know the law of connection completely before they seek. Answer these questions to yourself: Are you connected exclusively to your goals? Are you connected exclusively to ones you love the most? Is your commitment exclusive?

Wherever you've planted the seed of "exclusiveness" prosperity and love have to present themselves.

Drop the word "inclusive" from your mind and bring in the magic of "exclusive."

There are two ways to look at life. One is as though nothing is a miracle; the other is as though everything is. – Albert Einstein

Let's explore the other way of living life.

The second story is the story told by the great Ramakrishna Paramhansa who was one of the pioneers of spiritual thinking in India. If you get a chance, read his book *The Gospel of Ramakrishna*. It's the best gift you can give yourself.

A poor man had built a house on a hill. It was only a mud hut, but he had built it with great labour. A few days after, there was a violent storm and the hut began to rock. The man became very anxious to save it and prayed to the god of the winds, "'O god of the winds, please don't wreck the house!" But the god of the winds paid no heed to his prayer.

The house was about to crash. Then he thought of a trick. He remembered that *Hanuman (the god of strength)* was the son of the god of the winds. At once he cried out with great earnestness: "O revered sir, please don't pull down the house. It belongs to Hanuman. I beseech you to protect it." But still the house continued to shake violently.

Nobody seemed to listen to his prayer. He repeated it many times, "Oh, this house belongs to Hanuman!' But the fury of the wind didn't abate. Then he remembered that Hanuman was the devoted servant of Rama (a revered Hindu god), whose younger brother was Lakshmana. Desperately the man prayed, crying aloud, "Oh, this house belongs to Lakshmana!" But that also failed to help matters.

So the man cried out as a last resort: "This is Rama's house. Don't break it down, O, god of the winds! I beseech you most humbly." But this too proved futile, and the house began to crash down.

Whereupon the man, who now had to save his own life, rushed out of it with the curse: "Let it go! This is the devil's own hut!"

In less than five minutes he had transferred the ownership of the house from the most revered god to the devil's own hut!

Look at the poverty of connection Bless the human thinking

Says Krishna: *The mighty being accepts nobody's sin nor merit. Knowledge is shrouded in ignorance so all living beings are deluded.*

You have to choose between the power of connection versus the poverty of limited thinking.

Exercise No 3

I have a simple exercise which can fuel your power of connection.

What is your first productive activity of your day? Please write it down. Now have your first productive activity to second placed to make room for something more refreshing and powerful to take the first spot.

As simple as that. This will quickly help fuel your power of connection.

Think about it.

My wife used to spend the first thirty minutes of her day making tea and then drinking it. I thought it wasn't a great start to the day but try as much as she can she kept doing it for five years.

I thought to myself what a failure my life would be if I can't help her get off to a flying start each day with all the knowledge that I possess.

I pondered over this dilemma for weeks and then came the discovery. Any habit that you do for a week's time stays with you for a month or longer. Any habit that you do for a month's time stays with you for a year or longer. Any habit that you do for a year's'time stays with you for five years and more.

So the trick is not to force out your first activity but to just move it to second place.. Forcing it out causes pressure. And that's is what I suggested to my wife. Move making tea and drinking tea to second place and replace it with something more spectacular.

This simple change worked big time. It's these small successes which fuel the power of connection.

My first 30 minutes is spent connecting with my higher self. To me it is the best investment I can ever make. How about you?

Enlightenment Seed No 4

Krishna reveals the secret of relationships between men and women

What are the fields of human energy and how does they affect the relationship between men and women? Krishna reveals: *The beginning of the universe is unmanifest, the middle is manifest, and the end is unmanifest, O Arjuna.*

The words unmanifest and manifest are very important to help us embrace the enlightenment code. Understand what unmanifest is, what manifest is, and how this effects your energy patterns and your relationship with your partner.

The unmanifest is God without form, or to put it in other words, vibrant energy which is formless. This energy can't be influenced by anything. It's complete in itself. It lacks nothing. At the beginning of a cycle of creation this umanifested energy begins to take form. Human beings, animals, stars planets and everything in this universe is manifested out of this energy. At the end of the cycle of creation everything that was created, everything that was manifested, is dissolved again into the unmanifest as energy. So the beginning and end is all energy without form. It's only in the middle that we deal with form. Krishna reveals that the beginning and the end represents your real nature and the middle phase is apparent and temporary.

All created things are deceiving and unstable and makes you forget your real nature, says Krishna. Krishna is all for divine connection. He never says don't indulge in love making. He never says to not associate with the opposite sex. But his message is clear. Don't crave love making.

Don't be attached to the opposite sex but instead remember your unmanifested nature. You'll love more and lust less. You'll live more and worry less.

So where does the relationship between men and women become confused? Is making love with your partner wrong? Does excessive love lead to wrong attachment? Is association with the opposite sex bad?

Krishna says all these questions are rubbish and don't make any sense. Don't waste your time in all these questions, urges Krishna. He reveals that human beings can never lust. He says it is impossible that the unmanifest in you can get attracted.

The unmanifest in you doesn't lose its power when you make love with your partner, Krishna points out. The unmanifest in you doesn't become affected when you get emotional with your partner. Krishna says the unmanifest in you isn't influenced by your association with the opposite sex.

So what then is purity? What is it that gets affected when men and women unite?

The Secret Yoga of Krishna

Reveals Krishna: *Confining the mind to the heart, fixing the life force in the crown intent on yoga one merges with the divine.*

You are the unmanifest, Krishna asserts. You are the energy. You are divine. You are complete. What makes you incomplete is your thoughts. The mind thinks and every thought which it thinks is limited by its very nature. The mind is essentially energy manifested in a limited form.

But thinking, in this sense, isn't a necessity, Krishna says. You should think only when it's necessary. Krishna further says that the mind by its very nature loves to wander and is restless. However, there are two places where the mind is calm and perfectly at peace with itself. These two places are your heart and the center of your eye brows. If you train yourself to position your mind in these centers you'll achieve the state of purity declared by sages. Thoughts won't affect you as your mind will be merged in the unmanifest.

Krishna reveals that purity has nothing to do with your actions. It has nothing to do with your thoughts. Purity is simply the art of allowing your energy to travel upwards towards the heart and to the center of your eye brows.

For centuries human minds have been influenced to believe that purity is attained by non-indulgence. That is nonsense, says Krishna. Purity has nothing to do with your body and mind. The nature of body and mind is to gravitate downwards. Purity isn't influenced by an action or thought. You're pure because you've discovered something in you which is pure by its very nature.

Krishna declares your energy is pure and the nature of your energy is to flow. The direction of your energy is determined by the nature of your thoughts. If your thoughts are influenced by the environment you'll discover that very soon your energy will start flowing downwards and associate itself with the body and the mind.

Take a look at all your daily activities. Most of your activities you'll discover are influenced by the environment you place it in. The people whom you meet, the places you visit, the books you read, the movies or videos you watch all influence your thinking. You might feel you're choosing your thoughts and making decisions but on close observation you'll discover that you don't choose your thoughts. The environment and your deep intention choose your thoughts and you simply execute it or struggle with them.

Ask yourself this simple question. "Can I live one day without being influenced by my own thoughts?" You'll discover that not only can you live one day but you can live a whole life without being influenced by your thoughts. You might find it difficult to begin with but it is very much possible.

Thoughts are powerful but they aren't real. You are real, the unmanifest in you is real. There is a saying "The mind of a fool is caught in thinking and not thinking but the wise man is of the nature of no thought for he or she thinks what is appropriate."

Krishna says don't start thinking because your mind is wandering from one object to another. Take a notepad and write three powerful thoughts which you would like to manifest and stick to it for a whole week or month. Choose your thoughts and don't get associated with them, says Krishna. Once you've chosen your goal in the form of thoughts, let them go. Allow your vibrant energy to help you fulfil your goal. When you allow your energy to firm up your intention and to seek a suitable environment your energy will help you fulfill your goals.

Where the mind wanders you can be sure that the energy is travelling downwards. Where the mind is calm and perfectly at peace with itself you can be sure that the energy is travelling upwards towards the center of your heart.

Krishna further reveals that if you make love with your partner when your mind is seated in your heart you won't become impure because you're connected to the unmanifest. However, Krishna warns that when you repeatedly start indulging in the activity of love-making or thoughts related to it gradually the energy patterns begin to gravitate downwards and before you realise your entire unmanifested energy at your disposal would be travelling downwards. The end result is your mind will begin to wander. You'll associate your mind to be your real nature and the thoughts that your mind thinks will drive your life.

You'll forget your divine nature, and fail to remember the umanifested in you. Your whole life would then be one of wrong association, says Krishna. Hence, discrimination is advised.

Driven by lust and anger filled with hypocrisy and pride, offering nominal worship not ordained by the scriptures such senseless fools persecute me dwelling within. Know them to be demoniac. declares Krishna.

Krishna says that when your energy travels downwards you're persecuting him dwelling within you. *I dwell in the heart of all beings causing them to revolve through Maya as if mounted on a machine,* adds Krishna

The seat of divinity is your heart and the center of your eye brows. When you allow your energy to travel upwards your mind automatically will be seated in these two places. Any other place you allow the mind to be seated in will force you to think thoughts which by their very nature is incomplete. When the mind is rested peacefully in the heart and the center of your eye brows your thoughts won't be subject to external influence. You'll feel a sense of completeness being associated with your spirit.

Fix your mind on me, let your understanding be absorbed in me, henceforth doubtless will you abide in me for you are dear to me.

Krishna says you only have to get one thing right. Allow your energy to travel upwards.

The message of Krishna doesn't foster prohibition . **Prohibition delays connection. Indulgence breeds ignorance about connection.** So what stimulates divine connection?

The Power of Subtle Observation

Acceptance of human weakness and remembrance of the strength of the spirit is the secret to embracing the spirit. When you lean towards the "idea of divine connection" you create an environment for increasing the vibration of the mind. As the vibration of your mind soars your power to observe the subtle grows dramatically. What starts of as an "idea of divine connection" begins to gather momentum and gradually takes the form of concrete words, symbols, developing into a strong mental attitude and culminating finally into the goal of human life. When this happens you'll no longer struggle with prohibition or crave for indulgence. You'll love more and lust less. You'll live more and worry less. You'll be divinely connected.

Dangers of implementation

Most people think that fixing your mind in the heart and in the center of your eye brows can be attained through meditation. The reality is only one out of one million people who attempt to meditate would be able to reach the goal. This has been proven through the ages. What does that mean? It means that meditation isn't the cause which enables you to achieve the goal of fixing the mind in your heart. It's something else. Something which has been the secret of all sages who achieved it. What is the secret? It is simple and straightforward.

Get up early in the morning and simply remember that your mind should be centred in your heart. Touch your heart and promise yourself that you'll allow your energy to travel upwards. That's it. You don't have to do anything else. Whenever you're disturbed during the day remind yourself that your energy is travelling downwards. Acknowledge and feel the energy travelling downwards and then simply close your eyes, touch your heart, and promise yourself that you'll allow your energy to travel upwards and feel your energy moving towards the center of your heart. Remain calm in the midst of storm, advises Krishna.

He who in the midst of intense activity is serenely calm and in the midst of calmness is intensely active is a Yogi, O Arjuna, declares Krishna.

The state of your mind will undergo a radical change. Your thought patterns will move away from things which attempt to influence it. You'll feel an inexpressible joy within. Something will fill you up from within- this will come to all who strive to practise the yoga of Krishna.

The science of energy travelling upwards has been discovered by sages and the concept surrounding it is called "chakras." There are thousands of books on the movement of chakras. Many think that by reading the books they'lll be able to have their energy flow upwards. Truth is you don't have to know anything about the chakras. Not a single thing. The more you stay away from the subject and practise what I said the quicker and faster your energy will travel upwards.

The majority of books written on chakras are written by people who have approached the subject intelligently.

Most of them, though, haven't had any experience in allowing their energy to travel upwards towards the heart. Stay away from conceptual knowledge and don't burden yourself with more concepts and knowledge. Get the essence of the yoga of Krishna. Move closer to him and allow your energy to travel upwards. It's easy if you keep it simple. It's achievable if you practise it daily. It will deliver instant results if your intention is genuine. Krishna loves you.

Towards all beings I am the same. I hate none nor hold anyone dear. Those who worship me with devotion live in me and I in them, declares Krishna.

Notes

Chapter 5

The Power To Influence Your Destiny.

I am death carrying all beings away. Of things yet to be I am the origin. Of women I am the fame, glory, speech, memory, intelligence, endurance and patience. – Krishna to Arjuna in the *Bhagavad Gita*.

In the first four chapters we talked about the "power of connection. In this chapter we're going to touch upon the "power of influencing your destiny."

I'm going to present two contrasting stories that will help you bridge the gap between your thoughts and your ultimate destiny.

The first one is the story of the great Indian poet and dramatist Kalidasa who has been termed the "Shakespeare of India." Most people aren't aware of the fact that Kalidasa was born more than a thousand years before Shakespeare. In fact, by the end of this story you might think that it's Shakespeare who should be called the "Kalidasa of Europe."

In the 4th century CE in northern India there lived a princess who was a very learned woman and a master in spirituality and right thinking. She possessed extraordinary oratory skills and her father, the king, found it very difficult to find a suitable match for her.

She promised her father that she would marry the man who defeated her in philosophical debate. Many wise men came but within minutes she would defeat and humiliate them in the debate. This was extremely disappointing to many of the scholars.

One day all of her defeated opponents got together and decided that it was time that the princess be taught a lesson. They hatched a plan to marry her to a stupid man to humble her.

After many days of searching they came to a small village in the outskirts of the kingdom. There was Kalidasa sitting on the branch of a tree, trying to saw it off. But he was sitting on the wrong end of the branch and when he sawed through it he fell down!

The opponents were delighted. There could be no one more stupid and dumb than Kalidasa. They explained their plan to project him as a wise man, He wouldn't have to open his mouth during the debate by maintaining that he was under a vow of silence. Instead he would communicate through body language and facial expressions.

Kalidasa was uncertain but these opponents, still smarting from their defeats, convinced him that he had nothing to lose and a lot to gain. And so the "dumb" man agreed.

The debate began. The princess, not to take advantage, also decided to use sign language. She raised her one finger up - which meant that everything manifests from that one symbol of Brahman-the universal soul.
  Kalidasa's reaction was spontaneous. He raised two fingers up. *If she can raise one I can raise two,* he thought.

The princess was inspired. She thought Kalidasa meant: *God exists both with form and without form. The unmanifest and manifest both are true.* She then raised her palm up which meant that creation is made up of five gross elements - space, air, fire, water and earth.

Kalidasa was angry as he thought she had raised her palm to slap him. He showed his fist in response.

The princess was delighted. She thought he meant all the five elements were forms of manifestation but in the end they return back to that one unmanifested state. The five fingers represented the five elements but when the palm was closed it represents the unmanifested state in the form of the fist. She fell down at the feet of Kalidasa, declaring that Kalidasa was indeed a great man and that she would marry him. Thus, amid great pomp and ceremony, Kalidasa and the princess were wed.

On their first night the plot of using Kalidasa as stupid was exposed and the princess was shattered. How could this happen to her! All her life she was dedicated to the goddess Saraswati (the god of learning). *How can I stay with an idiot for the rest of my life?* she pleaded to God.

She insulted Kalidasa so badly that he wanted to end his life. He went to the nearby river to drown himself. Completely disgusted and frustrated, and finding no meaning in life, he was ready to give up his frail body. But then he noticed something very interesting. Local women were washing clothes on the edge of the river bank. He observed that the stones which the women were pounding the clothes were smooth and rounded, while the other stones in the vicinity were rough and ragged.

It was an epiphany for Kalidasa as it dawned to him that if stones which were so hard could change their shape by being pounded upon by clothes, then why wouldn't his dumb mind change if it was inspired by a fresh wave of knowledge!

The temple bell rang in the vicinity. It was the temple of Kali (the dreaded feminine God) which makes wishes come true. Inspired, Kalidasa prostrated before the goddess Kali and the rest is history.

Legend has it that the goddess Kali manifested herself before Kalidasa and wrote the syllable "Aum" in his tongue. From that day the dumb Kalidasa no longer existed. A world renowned poet and dramatist was born. Everything that he wrote about from then on has made him a famous writer. His most renowned play is *Shakuntala*.

What was the tipping point for Kalidasa?

How could a fool gain all the wisdom in the world by one simple observation? Is that possible?

Says Krishna: *Of things yet to be I am the origin That which we call destiny is the experiences* which are waiting to be explored...

The one event which brings the twist of fates is not the real game changer. The dumb Kalidasa was not really dumb.. He was only going through a state of stupidity as a result of his past impressions. The past is infinite, not finite. It isn't restricted to how far you can remember your past. Your memory is not an indication of your time of existence.

Those who think that our life begins when we take birth and ends when we die are equal to those who might be thinking that there will be only one spring, one fall, one winter, and one summer. Everything in nature follows a cycle.

The poet and dramatist existed deep within the dumb Kalidasa

What you see in the surface is not what is cooking deep within. Kalidasa had earned his right to being wise. His time for fame and glory started when the time for his state of stupidity ended. You might be just one day away from reaching your goal; you never know.

Don't be fooled by your current circumstances and your present pattern of thoughts

The thoughts that you're thinking today are what you intended to think many years back.

The gap between intention and event is far and wide and hence we don't understand the word destiny.

What you think and intend today is going to shape your destiny tomorrow. Never forget that you have something within you which is great and divine. You might have done all the hard work already. All you need is to remember and acknowledge the seed of transformation, the gigantic spirit lying dormant within you. A wise Kalidasa within you is waiting to explode. Allow yourself that privilege today.

The law of karma has its own way of making things happen.

Let's move to the second story.

This is the story of the king Harishchandra who was the 36th king who ruled India. He had two unique qualities. The first was that he never went back on his promise, and the other that he never uttered a lie. All the people in his kingdom respected him and he took great care of his subjects.

In India all kings trace their lineage to a sage. The king Harishchandra traced his to sage Vishwamitra. One day the revered sage Vishwamitra walked into his palace and reminded him of a promise which the king had made to him many years ago when the sage had helped him to solve a major problem.

Harishchandra had long forgotten about his promise but the sage Vishwamitra had other intentions that day. "I want you to donate your entire kingdom to me, O King," said Vishwamitra.

Harishchandra, dutiful as ever, duly handed over the kingdom to the sage and prepared to leave with his wife and son to Varanasi, a holy place in northern India. But before he departed there was more misery in store. The sage reminded him that an act of donation was deemed complete only when an additional honorarium was paid to him. Harishchandra had no money left to pay the additional amount of fees to the sage. But the promise had to be kept at any cost.

So he rented his wife and son to a noble family to work as helpers to pay for the additional amount. The money collected didn't suffice for the purpose and so the king rented himself to be a guard at a cremation ground in charge of collecting taxes for bodies to be cremated. But more misery was to follow.

One day when Harishchandra's son was plucking flowers for his master's prayer he was bitten by a snake and he died instantly. His mother carried his body to the cremation ground. His wife had no clue that Harishchandra was working there and he couldn't recognise his wife and dead son because of their ragged attire. In his sunken state of mind he refused to cremate the body of his son. His wife had no money to pay for the taxes needed to cremate their son. Harishchandra told her to sell the gold chain which she was wearing to cremate the boy's body. The gold chain which his wife was wearing was very dear to her. Called *mangalsutra* in India it's worn by all married women. It symbolizes the divine connection between husbands and wives.

When she removed the chain and handed it to him Harishchandra immediately recognised his wife and son. He was pained by the death of his child.

But the test of truth hadn't ended yet.

Harishchandra could cremate the body only after she paid the tax as he was duty bound. So he asked his wife to stand by him in the hour of calamity and give him any other possession instead of the gold chain to pay for the taxes. His faithful wife agreed. She had one last possession left. Her dress, called a saree in India. One part of it was used to cover the dead body of her son. She offered him the other half of the dress to pay the tax to perform the last rites.

When she proceeded to remove her dress destiny intervened. The sage Vishwamitra and all the gods in heaven manifested themselves and praised Harishchandra for his steadfast resolution to hold on to the principles of truth. They brought his son back to life and offered him and his wife a place in the kingdom of heaven.

Harishchandra refused to accept the invitation stating he can't leave the people of his kingdom and enjoy the world of heaven. The gods of heaven reminded him that the people of his kingdom are bound by the law of karma and have to continue their grind on earth but Harishchandra refused to accept the position.

He was ready to trade all his pious karma if that could help the people of his kingdom attain the world of heaven. Left with no other choice the gods agreed.

The story of Harishchandra has inspired thousands of people all over the world to stick to the path of truth.

The law of karma has happy endings, provided you know the law.

The twist of fates: a fool who became a world famous writer, and a king who had to stand the test of time and truth to move beyond the horizon.

Says Swami Abhedananda:

By seeing the seed of a banyan tree, one who has never seen the tree cannot imagine what powers lie dormant in it. When a baby is born we cannot tell whether he/she will be a great saint, or a wonderful artist, or a philosopher, or an idiot, or a villain of the worst type. Parents know nothing about their future. Along with the child's growth certain latent powers gradually begin to manifest. Those powers which are the strongest and most powerful will overcome others and check their course for some time, but when the powers that remain subdued by stronger ones get favorable conditions they will appear in manifested forms.

As for instance chemical forces may slumber in matter for thousand years but when the contact with the reagents sets them free, they appear again and produce certain results. For thousands of years galvanism slumbered in copper and zinc, which lay quietly beside silver. As soon as all three are brought together under the required conditions silver is consumed in flame.

Are you aware of your latent powers? Have you taken the time to explore and get in touch with it?

Are you prepared for the advent of the "favourable condition" which is going to change your destiny?

Exercise No 4

Let's do a simple exercise. Imagine the following scene.

You're travelling in a train to a particular destination. En route the train stops at stations. You get off the train, eat snacks, and board the train again. The journey continues...

Some of your co-passengers in the train are kind and gentle while others are horrible. You have no choice. You're all holed up in one compartment. The journey continues...

As the train speeds its way you wonder if you're headed in the right direction At the next station you get off and don't want to continue your journey. But at the last moment, as the train is leaving, you reboard. The journey continues...

Now you wonder how and when the journey started. Finally, you decide you're going to get off at the next stop and not board the train again. The train stops . You get off the train...

Now close your eyes and imagine whether you would have boarded the train again or taken a different path?

Enjoy the journey. The law of karma has happy endings.

Remember the saying: "Everything will be ok in the end. If it is not ok, then it is not the end"

I look behind and after

and find everything is right

In the deepest sorrows

I find a soul of light.

By Swami Vivekananda

Enlightenment Seed No 5

Follow Krishna's winning strategy to fulfil all your desires

Whosoever does my works, making me his supreme goal, becomes my devotee. Rid of all attachments, and without hatred towards others he effortlessly reaches me, O Arjuna.

Krishna reveals the secret of work. First, be inspired, urges Krishna. The will to be inspired is the key to great work. Spend more time knowing your field of action. For example, if you want to build a temple the will to build a temple should be more predominant in you than how to build the temple. The "why" is more important than the "how" to accomplish your desires.

Quick is the success born of works. reveals Krishna.

Krishna declares that if you have a feeling that you're not successful in what you're doing it means you're not inspired. Success comes easily to one who is inspired. There's a big difference between desire and success, states Krishna.

Desire drains away your energy. It forces you to work in a particular direction. Desire causes a dent in clear thinking. Success is healthy when it's devoid of desires.

When you're inspired success becomes a deep feeling and a wonderful experience which you carry with you. When you're not inspired success becomes an objective thing and generates desires which force you to work in a particular direction.

What then is inspiration?

Inspiration is simply a will to hold on to a higher level of vibration of mind

We talked about that in the earlier chapter of holding on to the "idea of a divine connection" and then gradually allowing this idea to take the form of a habit, a resolution, a strong mental attitude, and finally culminating into an intense goal. As you progress in this direction you'll notice the upward movement of your divine energy.

Reveals Krishna: *Knowledge is superior to repeated efforts. Superior to knowledge is meditation. Superior to meditation is renunciation of the fruits of action. This renunciation O Arjuna wins one peace immediately.*

Try this simple exercise. Take a notepad and write at least five powerful points on how you can organize your routine tasks more efficiently so that you find more free time for yourself. You can write about the routine tasks at work or at home or any other place you want to revamp. Do this exercise everyday first thing in the morning for ten minutes. Every day come up with new ideas which you can implement or refine the ideas of the previous day. If you do this exercise with a lot of interest you'll soon discover that by the end of the second week you would have achieved what is termed as "Inspiration."

Take a topic and leave everything else aside and put your mind body and soul into that area of interest. Approach it strategically and systematically without being emotional. In this way you would have allowed your mind to travel at a higher vibration and to tap into the unmanifested energy lying dormant within you.

Krishna further reveals that as you become successful in your work you'll soon realise that you've become attached to your work. So Krishna advises us to practise the art of detachment. He says there's no harm in being attached to something so long as you reserve the right to detach yourself from it.

What is detachment?

Detachment is simply the joy of having a mind which is full of energy, completely alert and peaceful with itself. A free mind has the will to travel beyond the desires of the body and mind and unite with the yoga of Krishna.

Grow up! says Krishna. Don't get caught up in work no matter how fancy and wonderful it might be. Widen your field of knowledge. Move beyond the desires of your mind and body. Increase the level of vibration of your mind. The nature of your spirit is to be detached. The nature of your mind and body is to be attached. Whenever Krishna lauds detachment he's referring to the spirit and not to mind and body activities. You can't be detached when you're in an "endless thinking mode."

Detachment is not the opposite of attachment, warns Krishna. Detachment is the power to enjoy the freedom of your spirit. Since we're attached we look upon detachment as a prohibition, something which we have to sacrifice or let go. However, that isn't the case.

Being attached is not the problem. Not being detached is the problem, says Krishna

How Great Minds Work

A man or a women who can work for five days, or even for five minutes without any selfish motive whatever without thinking of the future, of heaven, of punishment of anything of the kind has in him the capacity to become a powerful moral giant.- Swami Vivekananda

Krishna reveals that the first step to great work is to be inspired. Once you're inspired choose your field of action. This is your goal. Once you've established your goal never think about it again. Simply work on the means which will lead you to the goal and when you've perfected the means the goal will manifest itself.

Thinking about your goal will only generate desires. It will not lead you to success.

Shift your focus from the goal and set your mind towards increasing the level of vibration of your mind. Prepare your mind to focus on the little steps which will lead you towards the goal. Every day work on increasing the level of vibration of your mind and feel inspired to execute one little step towards the direction of your goal.

Krishna further reveals: *In Karma Yoga, there is no loss of good beginnings, one does not incur sin through error, even a little application of this yoga sets one free.*

In karma yoga there's no loss of good beginnings. Pay attention to the words no "loss of good beginnings."
What Krishna wants to reveal is this: The past is significant only for judging others. The past is insignificant when it comes to knowing your real nature.
If you've been a failure or if you haven't had great success till yesterday that doesn't stop you from tapping the unmanifested energy lying dormant within you. The connection is always open,

Says Krishna: *I never penalise you for your past. Your own past thoughts act as an obstacle, not me. You are free to unite with me anytime.*

Arjuna asks an important question to Krishna: "The mind is indeed fickle, O Krishna, and it wanders. I find its control more difficult than controlling the wind. How can I bring this mind under control, O Krishna?"

Krishna responds: *Doubtless, O hero! The mind is fickle and difficult to control but by means of practise and detachment it can be held in check. He whose self is uncontrolled yoga is hard to achieve. On the contrary my yoga is easy for one who has disciplined it by appropriate means, O Arjuna."*

Start today. Start right now is Krishna's simple message. Remember Krishna's dictum: *I never penalise you for your past. Your own past thoughts act as an obstacle not me. You are free to unite with me anytime. To the single minded yogin in perpetual communion with me I am always easily accessible, O Arjuna"*

I would encourage you to read the poem "Peace" by Swami Vivekananda which I've reproduced below.

Peace

Behold, it comes in might,
The power that is not power,
The light that is in darkness,
The shade in dazzling light.

It is joy that never spoke,
And grief unfelt, profound,
Immortal life unlived,
Eternal death unmourned.

It is not joy nor sorrow,
But that which is between,
It is not night nor morrow,
But that which joins them in.

It is sweet rest in music;
And pause in sacred art;
The silence between speaking;

Between two fits of passion --
It is the calm of heart.

It is beauty never seen,
And love that stands alone,
It is song that lives un-sung,
And knowledge never known.

It is death between two lives,
And lull between two storms,
The void whence rose creation,
And that where it returns.

To it the tear-drop goes,
To spread the smiling form
It is the Goal of Life,
And Peace -- its only home!

Notes

Chapter 6

Dancing With Maya (Illusion)

God is in the heart of all beings causing them to revolve through Maya as if mounted on a machine, O Arjuna. (Krishna said to Arjuna in the *Bhagavad Gita*)

In the first four chapters we talked about the "power of connection" and in the fifth chapter we touched upon "the twist of fates." In this chapter we'll discover the sometimes confusing word "Maya" and how you can literally at the snap of your finger raise your level of consciousness a million fold.

Says Krishna to Arjun: *Veiled by the delusive power of Yoga-maya I do not stand revealed to all. The deluded do not know me unborn and immutable.*

Let's begin with a story.

The sage Narada once said to Krishna, "Lord, explain to me what is Maya (illusion)"

A few days later, Krishna asked Narada to make a trip with him toward the desert. They walked several miles together, at which point, Krishna said, "Narada, I'm thirsty. Can you fetch some water for me?"

"I'll go at once, sir, and get you water."

A short distance away, there was a village. Narada entered the village in search of water and knocked at a door. A beautiful young woman opened it. At the sight of this woman, Narada immediately forgot that his Master was waiting for water – that he was perhaps even dying for the want of it. Narada forgot everything and stayed with the woman all day. Their meeting ripened into love and Narada asked the woman's father for her hand. Narada and the woman married, stayed in the village, and had children.

Twelve years passed.

Narada's father- in- law died and Narada inherited his property. He lived what he believed was a very happy life with his wife, his children, his fields, his cattle, and everything else he'd acquired.

Then one night the river rose until it overflowed its banks and flooded the entire village. Houses fell and the torrent of water drowned people and animals. Narada tried to escape with his wife and children, carrying one child on his shoulders. After a few steps, the current overwhelmed him. The child on his shoulders fell and was borne away.

A cry of despair came from Narada. In trying to save that child, he lost his grasp on his other child, losing this one as well. At last, the current took his wife, whom he had been clasping with all his might. The water threw Narada on the bank and he lay there, weeping and wailing.

Behind him, there came the gentle voice of Lord Krishna. He tapped him on his shoulders and said "My child, where is the water? You went to fetch a pitcher of water and I.m waiting for you. You've been gone for nearly fifteen minutes."

"Fifteen Minutes?" Narada exclaimed.

Twelve years had passed through his mind and yet all of this occurred in fifteen minutes. That is Maya. That is illusion.

"Where's my jug of water?" Krishna asked again.

"Well, you see, I was about to do that but ....."

Krishna remained insistent. "Where's my jug of water?"

Crestfallen, Narada had no answer.

Krishna then smiled and hugged Narada warmly. "I'm sorry, my child," he said, "but you need to go back from where you came. You need to start again. You need to go get the jug of water."

The jug of water is your purpose of life. It's easy to lose yourself on the way to finding the jug. How much easier would it be if a higher force in the universe could guide you towards it?

God is in the heart of all beings causing them to revolve through maya as if mounted on a machine, says Krishna.

The World's Greatest Discovery --- Maya

In my earlier book "The Secret of Bhagavad Gita" I touched upon four parallel worlds - The earth world, the lunar sphere, the electric sphere , the *Brahma lok(the highest vibration of mind),* and the world of Krishna.

Think about it. How could 12 years of sage Narada's life be equal to only 15 minutes of Krishna's time? Was Krishna joking when he said that?

Certainly not. Let's take an example. If you were to walk from New York to San Francisco, how much time would it take? Perhaps as much as 30 days or more. If you were to drive from New York to San Francisco how much time would it take? Probably you could do it in two days or less. What if you took a flight from New York to San

Francisco how much time would that take? No more than an hour.

What does all this mean?

Time is an illusion. The "vehicle" you use determines the duration of time.

The vehicle which Narada used was the mind with a very low vibration and the vehicle which Krishna employed was a mind with a very high vibration. It's very important that you understand this completely.

Does it make any sense if someone tells you it took him 30 days to walk from New York to San Francisco?

You might think that guy is crazy. He could have driven or taken a flight.

Time is insignificant once you gain the ability to change your vehicle. If you're at a low vibration you struggle with managing time and getting organised. However, if you're able to raise your vibration you hop on to a better vehicle and you don't have to worry about managing time because you're far ahead of the curve. You've mastered the science of perfect timing.

Twelve years at a low vibration of mind is equal to 15 minutes at a high vibration of mind. (12 years = 15 minutes)

Do a small exercise to prove this point. Flash back into the last twelve years of your life. Remember all the past events of your last twelve years, both good and bad.

How long can you keep your mind in the past 12 years? One minute or one hour? Or one day, or one year, or 12 years?

No matter how sensational or boring your past twelve years might have been you're not likely to remain in it for more than 15 minutes. In 15 minutes you can summarize your past 12 years. Your past 12 years is actually equal to only 15 minutes.

When you lived these 12 years you were under the influence of time and so your mind was at a low vibration. When you look back at your past your mind is more mature in relation to time and your higher mind is able to live in it for only fifteen minutes.

Real time is only 15 minutes

The rest is maya - illusion (12yrs less 15 minutes)
If Einstein would have derived an equation for Maya (Illusion)it might have been : Maya = Actual Time spent − Sum total of the experiences carried forward

Maya = 12years (Actual time spent) − 15 minutes (Experiences carried forward)

Think about it. How are you going to spend the next 12 years of your time? Which vehicle are you going to use to measure time?

If your mind is at a low vibration you'll be spending 11 years, 364 days, 23 hours and forty five minutes (12years less 15 minutes) under the influence of maya. If your mind is at a high vibration the same duration will be lived in 15 minutes.

Which way do you want to take your mind to?

Your past 12 years is worth only 15 minutes and your next 12 years would also be worth only 15 minutes.

Says Swami Vivekananda: *I was once traveling in the desert in India. I traveled for over a month and always found the most beautiful landscapes before me, beautiful lakes and all that. One day I was very thirsty and I wanted to have a drink at one of these lakes; but when I approached that lake it vanished.*

Immediately a blow came into my brain the idea that this was a mirage about which I had read all my life; and then I remembered and smiled at my folly, that for the last month all the beautiful landscapes and lakes I had been seeing were this mirage, but I could not distinguish them then.

The next morning I again began my march; there was the lake and the landscape, but with it immediately came the idea, "This is a mirage." Once known it had lost its power of illusion. So this illusion of the universe will break one day. The whole of this will vanish, melt away. This is realization.

So it is with the universe. We are all traveling in this mirage of the world day after day, month after month, year after year, not knowing that it is a mirage. One day it will break up, but it will come back again, the body has to remain under the power of past Karma (intentions and impressions), and so the mirage will come back.

This world will come back upon us so long as we're bound by Karma: men, women, animals, plants, our attachments and duties, all will come back to us, but not with the same power. Under the influence of the new knowledge the strength of Karma will be broken, and its poison will be lost. It becomes transformed for along with it there comes the idea that we know it now, that the sharp distinction between the reality and the mirage has been known.

The lesson is that you shouldn't forget the jug of water. Raise your level of vibration. You have 15 minutes to live in the next 12 years.

Exercise No 5

Print this and paste it in your drawing room.

Twelve is the magic number for personal transformation

I can master any characteristic trait and embrace it as a part of my personality in less than 12 years.

Love, purity, sacrifice, courage, honesty, integrity, discipline, holistic business skills, spiritual strategies - all this comes full circle at the end of 12 years. It takes 12 years to become a catalyst for change.

Step 1) Fast forward the calendar 12 years later. What would you love to master and be an expert in? Visualise your catalyst of change.

Step 2) Say to yourself "I will plant the seed now. I will nurture and protect it and keep growing it no matter how horrible my current circumstances are. If I can continue to raise my vibration of mind and hold on for 12 years all my obstacles will eventually give way. I'll never forget this proven spiritual strategy. I'll always remember that 12 is the magic number for personal transformation.

Enlightenment Seed No 6

Read this poem "No one to blame" by Swami Vivekananda

The sun goes down, its crimson rays
Light up the dying day;
A startled glance I throw behind
And count my triumph shame;
No one but me to blame.

Each day my life I make or mar,
Each deed begets its kind,
Good good, bad bad, the tide once set
No one can stop or stem;
No one but me to blame.

I am my own embodied past;
Therein the plan was made;
The will, the thought, to that conform,
To that the outer frame;
No one but me to blame.

Love comes reflected back as love,
Hate breeds more fierce hate,
They mete their measures, lay on me
Through life and death their claim;
No one but me to blame.

I cast off fear and vain remorse,
I feel my Karma's sway
I face the ghosts my deeds have raised —
Joy, sorrow, censure, fame;
No one but me to blame.

Good, bad, love, hate, and pleasure, pain

Forever linked go,
I dream of pleasure without pain,
It never, never came;
No one but me to blame.

I give up hate, I give up love,
My thirst for life is gone;
Eternal death is what I want,
Nirvanam goes life's flame;
No one is left to blame.

One only man, one only God, one ever perfect soul,
One only sage who ever scorned the dark and dubious ways,
One only man who dared think and dared show the goal
— That death is curse, and so is life, and best when stops to be.
Om Nama Bhagavate Sambuddhâya
Om, I salute the God, the awakened.

Notes

Chapter 7

Kill The Old Mind

That which the ignorant call as renunciation O Arjuna the wise know it to be my yoga. None who had discarded all mental constructions scales to the peak of yoga.

In the last chapter we discovered the dreaded word "Maya." In this chapter we'll discuss "the influence of experiences" and how we allow our experiences - both good and bad - to manufacture what sages call "Ignorance of the thinking mind."

Says Krishna to Arjun: *Knowledge is superior to repeated efforts. Superior to knowledge is meditation. Superior to meditation is renunciation of the fruits of action. This renunciation, O Arjuna, wins one peace immediately.*

Let's begin with a story.

In ancient northern India there lived King Bharthari. He was very interested in the higher aspects of human personality and he had a sage who advised him on spiritual matters.

Once King Bharthari asked his sage, "Why is the mind so fickle and unsteady?"

The sage laughed. "Listen, O King, to this story."

Karna, one of the prodigious warriors in the great epic, *Mahabharata,* was considered a "Dhan-veer" which means one who is ready to give up his possessions at a moment's notice.

One day as Karna was preparing himself to bathe by the river side a monk came to him and asked for alms. Karna requested him to wait for 15 minutes as it's a usual practise to first bathe and then give alms to the monks.

However, the monk said he was in a hurry and he couldn't wait. Karna didn't not want to disappoint the monk and so he took off the gold chain he was wearing and offered it with his left hand to the monk.

The monk refused to accept the gift saying that all offerings should be made with the right hand. Now Karna had oil applied in his right hand and so he had used his left hand to offer the chain.

The monk reminded Karna that he wouldn't get the benefits of charity if he presented the chain with his left hand.

Karna was a man of subtle mind as well as a great warrior and so he replied, "O monk, it might be true that the gods in heaven will not be pleased with my act of charity and not bless me but I have to remind you that my mind can change as I transfer the gold chain from my left hand to the right. Chances are I might reconsider giving you the gold chain as a gift of charity and you might not get it. So, O monk, please accept this offer even though I might not be benefited with this charity."

Saying so Karna gave the gold chain with his lefthand and the monk left.

King Bharthari was enlightened. He recalled how on many occasions he had changed his mind in split seconds on important decisions.

"But why do we fail to notice the fickleness of the mind and keep making mistakes, O sage. Why does this happen?"

The sage smiled.

Listen, O King, to this story.

There was an intelligent man who made a wealthy living by transporting charcoal from one border to another. Here is how he did it. Every day he would carry a huge bag of charcoal on a bicycle from one border to another. There was strict security in the border and everything was thoroughly checked. The security guards used to get very irritated when this little man would walk in because they had to check his entire bag of charcoal. Every day they checked his bag of charcoal and found nothing improper.

The next day in the early morning the charcoal deal would return to his home town, and in the evening he would again go to the border with his big bag of charcoal on the bicycle. This continued for months.

One day one of the security guards, when he was off duty, found this charcoal dealer drinking tea in a restaurant. Both men recognised each other and the charcoal dealer invited the guard to join him for a cup of tea.

The guard accepted the invitation. "So what do you do with the bag of charcoal? I always wanted to ask you. How do you make a living selling these bags of charcoal?"

The charcoal dealer smiled. "I'll tell you a little secret but keep it to yourself. I don't sell the bag of charcoal beyond the border. I sell the bicycle. There's a great demand there for bicycles."

The charcoal dealer explained how he would take a new bicycle and sell it for a fine profit. But he wouldn't have been able to do that without the bag of charcoal on the top of the bicycle. The security guards wouldn't have allowed the bicycle to be taken as an item to be sold. In this fashion, the bags of charcoal helped him to sell the bicycles and become rich.

In a similar manner, O King, our mind is the bag of charcoal. It takes us from one place to another, one desire after another. We fail to notice it like the security guards who failed to notice or understand the charcoal dealer's real intention. Your spirit is the only thing that's real. The power of your mind is borrowed from the spirit. When you're not alert you pay too much attention to your mind and the bag of charcoal; when you're alert you focus only on the spirit - the bicycle.

King Bharthari was enlightened.

"So what is the secret code for life, O sage."

The sage smiled. As he had performed lots of austerities and penance he had been awarded the fruit of immortality by the gods of heaven. Since he was serving as the king's advisor he gifted the fruit of immortality to the king.

"Take this, O King. This is the secret code. Keep this fruit with you. You'll find it useful."

Later that night the king thought: *The sage has already enlightened me. I don't need this fruit. I'll gift this to my beautiful wife.*

He summoned his wife, and explained to her about the gift he was giving her.

It so happened that his wife was fond of a charioteer who used to take the queen all over the city. She thought: *I don't need this fruit. It might help the charioteer.* So she gave the fruit as a gift to the charioteer.

The charioteer used to visit a prostitute on a regular basis and he thought: *I don't need this fruit. It will help her.* So in one of his meetings he gifted the precious fruit to the prostitute.

The prostitute was delighted. She wasn't aware of the journey of the fruit from the king to the queen to the charioteer and finally to her. She thought: *What will I do with it. The king is the best person who deserves it.* And so next day she went to the court of the king and presented the fruit to King Bharthari.

King Bharthari fell at the feet of the prostitute and left the kingdom, and his wife, never to return. He became one of the greatest sages of ancient India.

Connecting the dots

What made King Bharthari quit his wife and kingdom and embrace the power of the spirit?

These stories shed light.

The story of Karna. The mind is fickle. Your mind can change in a split second. Try transferring a gold chain from the left hand to the right hand and observe the workings of the mind.

The story of the charcoal dealer. The security guards were focused on searching the bag of charcoal, which the dealer realized. Your mind is aware that when you're at a low vibration it can feed you anything.

Like the security guards you'll be searching the bag of charcoal and blaming events, circumstances, and people for your impressions. When you're at a high vibration you focus only on the spirit and allow it to form experiences for you.

The incident of the prostitute returning back the fruit he had so lovingly presented to his wife reveals that what you give comes back to you - both good and bad. **The duration of relationships have nothing to do with the depth of the relationships.**

King Bharthari had learned the greatest secret: the relationship with the spirit has the highest value. The depth of the relationship with the spirit is unmatched. No object, person or event can match the depth of your relationship with the spirit.

The ignorant might conclude that King Bharthari had renounced his kingdom and left everything. But that isn't true.

King Bharthari had connected the dots that led him to the supreme knowledge. The yoga of Krishna is the only way to live a great life.. He realised his basic mistake.

Experiences shouldn't lead you to knowledge..

It's knowledge that should help you to form great experiences. Knowledge of the spirit is complete. If you try to know more about your spirit through the experiences of your life you would be like the security guard who would have always wondered what the charcoal dealer was up to carrying the bag of charcoal in his bicycle.

Knowledge of the spirit is complete.. Experiences will always leave you with a desire to know something more.

First know, then think, then act, and finally experience. Don't make the mistake of knowing the spirit through events and circumstances. You'll be selling your spirit short. Your knowledge would be one sided.

Always remember: *Him the fire cannot burn, the water cannot wet, the wind cannot dry.*

The purusha (the spirit) isn't influenced by change. You have to simply embrace it, not know it through experience. You have to know it as it is.

You have to connect the dots through the yoga of Krishna

All knowledge manifests from the spirit and so all your experiences should be experiences of your soul. No experience belongs to you. All experiences are returned back to the spirit. So don't be too much carried away by good and bad experiences.

King Bharthari didn't renounce his kingdom and wife. He left to practise the yoga of Krishna.

That which the ignorant call as renunciation O Arjuna the wise know it to be my yoga. None who had discarded all mental constructions scales to the peak of yoga, O Arjuna.

Connect the dots! Practise the yoga of Krishna!

Enlightenment Seed No 7

Read this poem "The Living God" by Swami Vivekananda

He who is in you and outside you,
Who works through all hands,
Who walks on all feet,
Whose body are all ye,
Him worship, and break all other idols!

He who is at once the high and low,
The sinner and the saint,
Both God and worm,
Him worship — visible, knowable, real, omnipresent,
Break all other idols!

In whom is neither past life
Nor future birth nor death,
In whom we always have been
And always shall be one,
Him worship. Break all other idols!

Ye fools! who neglect the living God,
And His infinite reflections with which the world is full.
While ye run after imaginary shadows,
That lead alone to fights and quarrels,
Him worship, the only visible!
Break all other idols!

Note: *The reference to "Break all other idols" in the poem above is* about *destroying the conflict in the mind in relation to the limited idea of god. Vivekananda urges us to expand and outgrow the "idea of God."*

Notes

Chapter 8

The Magic of the Ecode

Keep saying, "I am free." Never mind if the next moment delusion comes and says, "I am bound." Dehypnotize the whole thing. – Swami Vivekananda.

Fair Warning: Please don't read this chapter if you haven't read the earlier chapters. You won't benefit from the Ecode.

In the first four chapters we talked about the "power of connection." In the fifth we touched upon "the twist of fates." In the sixth and seventh chapters we discussed the often misunderstood concept of "Maya" and how it influences your experiences. In this chapter we'll cover the enlightenment code whose essence genuine spiritual seekers spend years seeking.

Sit back and enjoy. It's going to be fun.

Says Krishna to Arjun: *He who knows the Purusha(spirit) and prakarti(it's power) is no longer born in this world no matter how he or she fares in this world.*

Krishna hands out the E-code to us in this dictum. Before I reveal the Ecode I want to take you through an adventurous journey. Let's start with a long but beautiful poem by Swami Vivekananda.

■ ı

O'ver hills and dale and mountain ranges

In the temples,churches and mosques,

In the Vedas, the Bible and The AlKoran

I have searched for Thee in vain...

Like a child in the wildest forest lost,

I have cried and cried alone,

Where art Thou gone, my Love, My God

And The Echo answered "Gone.." "Gone"...

And days and nights and years then passed

A fire was in the brain,

I knew not when day changed in night

The heart seemed rent in twain.

I laid me down on Ganges shore

Exposed to sun and rain,

With burning tears I laid the dust

And wailed with waters roar.

I called on all the holy names

Of very clime and creed

"Show me the way in mercy, ye

Great ones who have reached the goal"

Years then passed in bitter cry

116

Each moment seemed an age,

Till one day midst my cries and groans

Some one seemed calling me...

A gentle soft and soothing voice

That said 'my son' 'my son'

That seemed to thrill in unison

With all the chords of my soul..

I stood on my feet and tried to find

The place the voice came from,

I searched and searched and turned to see

Round me, before and behind

Again and again it seemed to speak

The voice divine in me.

In rupture, the soul was hushed

Entranced , Enthralled in bliss

A flash illumined all my soul,

The heart of my heart opened wide

O joy of bliss, what do I find

My love, my love you are here

And you are here, my love my all !

And I was searching thee

From all eternity you were there

Enthroned in majesty !

From that day forth wherever I roam

I feel Him standing by

O'ver hill and dale and mountain ranges

Far far away and high...

The moon's soft light, the stars so bright

The glorious orb of the day

He shines in them, His beauty might-

Reflected lights are they

The majestic morning, The melting evening,

The boundless billowy sea,

In nature's beauty, song of the birds

You will see through them it is He.

Thou speakest in the mothers lay

That shuts the babies eye,

When innocent children laugh and play

You will see thee standing by...

When holy friendship shakes the hands

He stands between them too,

He pours the nectar in mothers kiss

And the baby's sweet mama..

Thou art my God with prophets old

All creeds do come from Thee

The vedas the bible and the Quran bold

All sing thee in harmony

Thou art, Thou art , The soul of souls

In the rushing stream of life,

Om Tat Sat OM, Thou Art my God,

My love I Am thine, I am thine....

****

Let's begin the journey for the Ecode. Imagine the following scene before you. You're walking through a dense forest and it will take you at least 10 days to reach your destination. You're very anxious and uncertain that you'll make it.

Two questions are of vital importance here.

1. Why are you travelling through the dense forest?
2. What forces you to believe that you have to experience anxiety and doubt for the next ten days in your journey through the forest?

The answer to the first question is obvious. You're travelling through the dense forest as a result of the law of karma. It's a higher law which connects various events and circumstances in a strange and unusual way to ensure that you go through certain experiences based on your past actions.

The law of karma is not biased

This is important to understand. The law of karma is on your side. It doesn't want to inflict pain on you. It simply provides you with an opportunity to grow based on your personality.

The law of karma wants you to experience certain emotions so that your knowledge is complete with regard to that experience. That's it. But here comes the funny part. For ages people have linked every cause to this law of karma. Everyone submitted themselves to the mercy of the law. The question was asked, "Is there an end to all this?"

The E- code

Think about it. If you had a vehicle and a map you could have crossed the dense forest in less than a day.

Let's make this more interesting. If you had an airplane you could have crossed the dense forest in less than ten minutes.

So what does this mean?

Here's the million dollar secret: The law of karma never says that you have to suffer for ten days. It simply says you have to go through this experience. If you have a superior vehicle you can pass through that same experience in less than ten minutes.

The vehicle which you're travelling through life is at a very low vibration and that's the reason you're never able to get out of the law of karma.

What can be experienced in 10 minutes is taking you 10 days

You can shrink time once you hop on to a superior vehicle. When you're grounded in the body and mind you'll continue to be influenced by the law of karma and you'll have to return back to this earth world again and again.

When you raise the vibration of your mind you can shrink time. The whole baggage of impressions which you're destined to experience over a number of life times in the future can be experienced over a period of less than a year.

You can be free in this birth.

When you're able to raise your vibration to the level of the Brahma lok(the highest vibration of mind) you conquer the law of karma because you have experienced all impressions in a very short time.

This is how great men and women have been able to dump their association with the law of karma. The law of karma will eat you up if you have a low vibration. The secret which Krishna handed over to Arjun was this:

> "He who knows the Purusha and the Prakarti is no longer born in this world no matter how he or she fares in this world."

All laws operate in certain fields.

Beyond that field they lose their power. The law of gravity works in the earth world. It doesn't function in higher worlds. The law of karma works through your body and mind when you're at a low vibration. When you're at a high vibration you change the field... and with it everything changes.

Says Krishna to Arjun: *He who know the field and knows me as the owner of the field knows me completely.*

How wise men and women wipe out the experiences of 100 lifetimes of Karma in less than seven days

We saw in chapter six that your last 12 years is equal to only 15 minutes of valid experiences carried forward. If you take this equation further a whole life time is worth only 90 minutes of experiences carried forward (this is assuming the average life span is 72 years and if 12 years is equal to 15 minutes of experience carried forward, 72 years is equal to 90 minutes of experiences carried forward).

You can shrink the experiences of the last 100 lifetimes and live those experiences which haven't fructified in less than seven days.

It's that powerful!

A 100 life times of Karma can be wiped out in less than seven days (100 lifetimes * 90 minutes per life time experiences carried forward = 9000 minutes = 6 ¼ days)

Wouldn't Einstein and all the ancient sages as well be thrilled with that equation?

Who said you can't be free in your life birth? You can be absolutely free no matter how horrible or how deep your karmic bonds are.

Think of the power you possess.

You can blow away 100 lifetimes of karma in less than seven days. By using a rusted vehicle you're simply allowing the law of karma to influence you for countless births.

The Evolution of Communication and How It Can Set You Free

Communication used to travel slowly in olden days because the vehicle of communication was lethargic. Once a superior vehicle of communication was used the duration was shortened. Just imagine if you had to convey your message to someone using the traditional approach of sending the message through a dove? How frustrated would you be today? From the dove we moved to horse to post to courier and now to instant communication via email and mobile phones.

What used to take one month is now communicated to the other person in less than a fraction of a second. A superior vehicle has extraordinary speed which shrinks time.

Wisdom should evolve not stagnate with time

We've allowed ancient wisdom to rust and become outdated by looking at it through our tiny frame of mind. To allow it to evolve you need to master the art of shrinking time. All logic, arguments, dialogues and reasoning bite their dust when you hop on to a superior vehicle using the yoga of Krishna.

What are the qualities of the superior vehicle?

Just one says Krishna. It should not be influenced by the three constituents of change. The agent of error (Tamas), the agent of equal opportunity (Rajas), and the agent of oneness (Sattvic).

The Three Agents of Change

No 1: Agent of error (Tamasic) – This agent forces you to view the part as the whole. Here's an example. One who enjoys eating apples will talk about it as if it was the only fruit existing on earth.

No 2: Agent of equal opportunity (Rajasic) – This agent forces you to respect and accept the individual existence of everything. One who enjoys eating an apple will also accept that a mango, banana, orange and every other fruit existing on earth has a justified existence.

No 3: Agent of oneness (Sattvic) – This agent forces you to discover unity in diversity. All fruits - apple, mango, banana orange and every other fruit - comes from the seed which is created by God.

These three agents of change exist in varying proportions in every being. They force one to think and act in a particular way resulting in mutual conflict and disharmony in the world.

There is no being in this world or in the world of heaven who is free from these three constituents, says Krishna.

The vibration of the earth world, heaven, and the electric world are all bound by constituents. They will force you to come back. The vibration at the Brahma lok is the only one which is free from constituents.

When you're free from the three constituents whatever you do doesn't rebound onto you. You no longer become the spider which casts its web around yourself. Your thoughts, actions and experiences are placed in a field which is self-destructive every moment. Nothing is carried forward. You're not bound by the law of karma. You're free!

What was destined to happen to you in this life time after 20 years you can allow to happen to you in the next 20 minutes. It's that powerful if you follow the E-code.

He who knows the Purusha and the Prakarti is no longer born in this world no matter how he or she fares in this world.

Abandon the old rusted vehicle which you've held on to your chest for ages. Hop on a superior vehicle. You'll no longer be born in this world. You'll be free as you've used the E-code. Simply raise the vibration of your mind all the way up to the Brahma lok (the highest vibration of mind possible). That's it in a nutshell!

Your journey is complete. Your quest is complete. Krishna has handed you the E-code. Accept it and live a great life!

Enlightenment seed No 8

Krishna reveals a simple fix to solve religious disharmony

Says Krishna to Arjun: Some marvel about it by beholding it, some marvel about it by talking about it, others marvel about it by hearing it, but even those who behold, talk or hear about me do not know me completely, O Arjuna.

Krishna adds: *I am the thread which runs through the pearls of all religions, O Arjuna.*

Krishna reveals the difference between truth and culture

The unmanifest is the truth says Krishna and the unmanifest can't be revealed through words, pictures and sounds. What is revealed through words, pictures, symbols and sounds is culture which helps you to remember truth.

All religions represent culture which enable you to remember truth

This is very important to understand as it can put an end to most of the irrational way of thinking about religions. *Swami Vivekananda adds:* Whoever thinks their religion is the best need to know that all the principles and tenets that they take pride in has in some form or other been discovered and preached millions of years before. Truth has always existed before religion. Religion is about culture which leads to truth. People have for centuries been mistaking culture to be truth . Dont do that, says Krishna.

Unity can only be found in laws. Prayers, meditation, rituals and worship reveal a higher law in existence. Pray to your heart's content but remember that when you pray, meditate or worship the god of your religion you're worshipping the unmanifest indirectly.

Embrace the unmanifest directly - not indirectly, says Krishna.

Those who are devotees of other divinities and who worship them with faith are worshipping me alone but not as per vedic injunctions. I am the master and enjoyer of all sacrifices but they lapse to understand. I am the maker of Vedanta and knower of all Vedas. By means of the Vedas I alone am to be known.

Krishna is very clear about divine connection. He says no matter which god you worship or pray to you're worshipping him indirectly. Embrace me directly, encourages Krishna.

When a Hindu offers prayers to Shiva or any other god in the Hindu pantheon he is worshipping me ignorantly, says Krishna. Similarly, when a Christian offers prayers to Jesus and a Muslim prays to Mohammed they are indirectly praying to Krishna.

I am the unmanifest, the highest law which runs this universe. The higher law of karma and time have manifested out of me, says Krishna.

He further adds: *Towards all beings I am the same I hate none nor hold anyone dear. Those who worship me with devotion live in me and I in them.*

Krishna is very clear that he isn't attached to any religion

He is the unmanifest. Religion was his idea, Krishna declares, but the understanding of each faith is up to the individual.

Religion was established to help remember truth, not become truth

Religion represents culture, not truth. It symbolizes all higher laws which can help you remember the unmanifest.

Religion should never be forced on anyone; rather the study of higher laws should be encouraged. That religion which attempts to convert a person from one religion to another is like the ass carrying a load of sandalwood only knows the weight and not the value of his burden.

If all human beings on earth followed one religion would that help humanity? Not at all.

What would raise humanity is when there is appreciation for the higher laws, when every human being has the will to unite with the unmanifest. The *Vedas*, the *Upanishads* and the *Bhagavad Gita* contains these higher laws.. Know them first and then follow the culture of your religion. You'll love your religion a thousand times more than you ever did.

Unity can only be found in laws and appreciation for the unity can only exist when there is freedom to explore these laws through varied cultures.

The *Bhagavad Gita* contains the laws which represent truth and the different religions represent human freedom in the form of culture to explore the grand truth.

Says Vivekananda : *The tree is known by its fruits. A mango fruit can manifest only out of a mango tree. An apple seed cannot give rise to a mango fruit. This is very important to understand. We all want peace and harmony in this world. We want people to be kind to us, to respect us and give us love and appreciation. We are dreaming of mango fruits but there are not sufficient mango trees in the environment to produce the mango fruits. We need to produce more men and women of greater character, beings who have a broad mind, who understand the laws of the spiritual world. Wherever thou finds a great soul trying to raise humanity know that he is born out my splendour, that I reside in Him. Whenever virtue subsides and irreligion prevails I manifest myself again and again.*

Krishna says that everything in nature is bound by law which means anything which is happening now has happened before and will happen in the future, too. Great men and women will emerge, wicked people will dominate for a while, and human emotions will prevail. Winter will change to spring and back to winter.

Goodness isn't a one time thing. It existed before and it will exist in the future.

There will arise more superior souls in the future. Make no mistake about that. Don't rush to conclusions, says Krishna. All great men such as Buddha, Christ, Mohammed, and the founders of all other religions aren't a one time thing. Great men and women will continue to rise in their own way at God's own will.

Krishna further reveals: *A mother recognises a child in whatever dress he comes. If she does not she is not the mother of the child. Recognise the greatness in you and marvel it in others whom you see it shining.*

Read this poem "The Song of the Free" by Swami Vivekananda

The wounded snake its hood unfurls,
The flame stirred up doth blaze,
The desert air resounds the calls
Of heart-struck lion's rage.

The cloud puts forth it deluge strength
When lightning cleaves its breast,
When the soul is stirred to its in most depth
Great ones unfold their best.

Let eyes grow dim and heart grow faint,
And friendship fail and love betray,
Let Fate its hundred horrors send,
And clotted darkness block the way.

All nature wear one angry frown,
To crush you out - still know, my soul,
You are Divine. March on and on,
Nor right nor left but to the goal.

Nor angel I, nor man, nor brute,
Nor body, mind, nor he nor she,
The books do stop in wonder mute
To tell my nature; I am He.

Before the sun, the moon, the earth,
Before the stars or comets free,
Before e'en time has had its birth,
I was, I am, and I will be.

The beauteous earth, the glorious sun,
The calm sweet moon, the spangled sky,
Causation's law do make them run;
They live in bonds, in bonds they die.

*And mind its mantle dreamy net
Cast o'er them all and holds them fast.
In warp and woof of thought are set,
Earth, hells, and heavens, or worst or best.*

*Know these are but the outer crust -
All space and time, all effect, cause.
I am beyond all sense, all thoughts,
The witness of the universe.*

*Not two nor many, 'tis but one,
And thus in me all me's I have;
I cannot hate, I cannot shun
Myself from me, I can but love.*

*Wake up from the dream, Break free from the bonds,
Be not afraid of the mystery,
My shadow, cannot frighten me,
Know once for all that I am He.*

Notes

132

....
....
....
....
....
....
....
....
....
....
....
....
....
....
....

Chapter 9

The Mystery of Life & How To Demystify It

The first step upwards is when we recognise ourselves as children of God. The last step is when we realise ourselves as the One, The Atman the soul.... – Swami Vivekananda

In this final chapter we will touch base upon the one mystical trait found common among all the great men and women. This is a quality you should add to your arsenal of life changing tools.

Says Krishna to Arjun: *He who perseveres imbued with yoga sees the jiva(soul) dwelling in the inner self while those of unpurified minds not having mastered their senses fail to see me despite perseverance.*

Pay careful attention to two words: perseverance and yoga.

Let's take an example to understand this verse from the master

A shoe-shine man used to work hard all day. He was honest, and a man of integrity. He had tremendous perseverance and treated his customers well.

Do you think the shoe-shiner will become rich just because he was honest, and had tremendous perseverance?

Absolutely not.

Perseverance only helps you to pursue the goal. It doesn't help you to reach the goal.

He would need something else to become rich. But the shoe-shiner had skills and a great work ethic. This combination gives him the confidence that he too can become rich if he could master the strategies of wealth building to expand his business.

Perseverance + Absence of Strategies = Pursuing the goal

Perseverance + Application of Strategies = Achieving the goal .

Krishna says there are four different paths to living a grand life.

The first is the path of knowledge called *Jnana Yoga*.

The second is the path of work called *Karma Yoga*.

The third is the path of devotion called *Bhakti Yoga*.

The fourth is the path of meditation called *Raja Yoga*.

There are countless discussions and arguments by various scholars of the past as to which of these four paths is the best.

Krishna is very clear. He says none of the four paths will help you reach Brahma lok (the highest vibration of mind possible) unless and until you combine the path with his yoga.

In addition, Krishna points out that just because you were a master at work and achieved great results doesn't mean you are spiritual. Most people on earth tend to believe that because they give to charity and have great work ethics they are spiritual. That is completely wrong! Giving to charity and having excellent work ethics are fine characteristics which should be followed by everyone; but spirituality has nothing to do with all this.

Spirituality happens when you combine work with yoga, Krishna says.

The key word is yoga, and by yoga I don't mean twisting your arms and legs around in different positions. That kind of yoga is different and great but it achieves a different purpose.

The yoga of Krishna is the catalyst which transforms everything that you do and places your thoughts and actions in a superior field where the law of karma and law of time doesn't operate.

Just because you pray every day and go to a church or temple doesn't mean you're spiritual. You become spiritual, Krishna relates, when you combine your devotion with yoga.

Just because you read the scriptures and are knowledgeable doesn't mean that you're spiritual. You have to combine your knowledge with yoga.

Just because you meditate and can read other people's mind and heal others doesn't mean you become a saint. You still have to combine your power of meditation with yoga.

The yoga of Krishna is the art of effortlessly increasing the vibration of the mind and operating at a superior level. Any action or thought performed at this level doesn't rebound to you. You become free the moment you master the art of transcendence.

Karma + Yoga= Karma Yoga

Jnana + Yoga = Jnana Yoga

Bhakti +Yoga = Bhakti Yoga

Raja + Yoga = Raja Yoga

Next time that you indulge in something mentally add "yoga of Krishna" to that activity and watch the result. Yoga is a trait which is the ideal combination of knowledge, love, and free will.

Imagine the following scene. You have a mango seed and you want a mango fruit manifested from this seed.

So what would you need?

You would need fertile land, the right soil, proper sunshine, rain, and many other ingredients. This right combination is referred to as the "proper environment" for the growth of the tiny mango seed into a full blown and juicy mango fruit.

Mango seed + Proper Environment = Mango fruit

The yoga of Krishna helps you create the right climate for achieving fast and quick results without getting caught in the mesh of the law of karma.

Step 1 - Increase the vibration of your mind.

Step 2 - When you've increased the vibration of your mind you've created the right climate for the transformation to happen.

Step 3 - Choose any path --work, love, meditation or knowledge - and mentally add "yoga of Krishna" to every thought or action.

Step 4 - Enjoy the result and revel in your new spirit.

Step 5 - Repeat steps 1 to 4

Says Krishna to Arjun: *He who perseveres imbued with yoga sees the jiva dwelling in the inner self while those of unpurified mind not having mastered their senses fail to see me despite perseverance.*

Perseverance + Ordinary vibration of mind = Craving, Doubt, Unsteady mind and Lack of fulfilment.

Perseverance + Yoga of Krishna = Completeness, Inspiration, touch of class, sense of fulfilment and the ability to express the freedom of the spirit.

Let me leave you with this wonderful story.

Once a king invited Krishna and Arjun (one of the great warriors in the *Mahabharata*) to his kingdom. On arrival the king couldn't greet them personally as he was busy in a meeting with some visiting dignitaries. He instructed his attendants to treat Krishna and Arjuna well and that he would see them in 30 minutes. One hour passed by and the king still didn't come to meet Krishna and Arjun.

Arjun got furious and thought it is time to teach the king a lesson. He was unhappy that Krishna wasn't greeted by the king personally and now had to wait for an hour for no reason. Krishna advised Arjun to be calm and said they would wait for another 15 minutes.

Fifteen minutes passed and the king still didn't come. Krishna called the attendant and left a message for the king that he would return back some other time and thanked him for the invitation.

Arjun was even more furious now when Krishna, in leaving the kingdom, blessed the king. "May all your desires be fulfilled."

Arjun asked Krishna why he blessed the king when he wasn't given proper treatment. Krishna advised him to be calm and said he would soon find out.

En route, Krishna visited one of his favourite devotees. This devotee was an ordinary person. His wife had died and he had a small son. He made his living by selling milk from two cows which he owned.

The devotee was thrilled to have Krishna as his guest. He served Krishna and Arjun joyfully for two weeks. Then Krishna and Arjun bade him goodbye.

In less than ten days after Krishna's departure the devotee's son and his two cows died.

Arjun was disturbed and asked Krishna for an explanation. "Why did you do that to that poor man? He served you so well and he's one of your favourite devotees. Still you took away everything from him while you blessed that idiot king who didn't even treat you properly."

Krishna replied: *I am death carrying all beings away. Of things yet to be I am the origin. I gave the king what he wanted. He was more interested in enjoying the world and so I wanted him to fulfill his desires quickly so that he could eventually develop an interest in the higher aspects of his personality. I gave the poor man what he wanted. He wanted to unite with me and his work and worldly responsibilities were causing a hindrance to him so I helped him remove the obstacle.*

Arjun digested this explanation. Then Krishna added:

He who knows me along with my manifestations in the elementals, the sacrifices and the divinities know me completely, O Arjuna. The mighty being accepts nobody's sin nor merit. Knowledge is shrouded in ignorance so all living beings are deluded. Towards all beings I am the same. I hate none nor hold anyone dear. He who worships me with devotion live in me and I in them. Where the yogin Krishna is there the warrior Arjun is. There dwells victory, prosperity and love.

Enlightenment Seed No 9

Read this poem " **Who Knows How Mother Plays?**" by Swami Vivekananda

Perchance a prophet thou-
Who knows? Who dares touch
The depths where Mother hides
Her silent failless bolts!

Perchance the child had glimpse
Of shades, behind the scenes,
With eager eyes and strained,
Quivering forms-ready
To jump in front and be
Events, resistless, strong.
Who knows but Mother, how,
And where, and when, they come?

Perchance the shining sage
Saw more than he could tell;
Who knows, what soul, and when,
The Mother makes Her throne?

What law would freedom bind?
What merit guide Her will,
Whose freak is greatest order,
Whose will resistless law?

To child may glories ope
Which father never dreamt;
May thousandfold in daughter
Her powers Mother store.

Notes

Glossary

- Purusha – the unmanifest, god without form, universal soul
- Jiva- the individual soul
- Prakarti – cosmic intelligence, idea of the universe
- Karma- the subtle law of cause and effect
- Tamasic- the agent of error
- Rajasic- the agent of equal opportunity
- Sattvic- the agent of oneness
- Brahma lok(the highest vibration of mind)
- Electric sphere, earth world, lunar sphere (the different parallel worlds representing the different vibration of mind)
- Maya- a higher intelligence which causes illusion in the mind
- Yoga of Krishna – the right environment which transforms thoughts into results. The yoga of Krishna is different from the physical yoga exercises taught all over the world.
- Vedas and Upanishads – revered Hindu scripture

Printed in Great Britain
by Amazon